WHAT A DAY THIS CAN BE!

WHAT
A
DAY
THIS
CAN
BE!

A CHRISTOPHER "Three-Minutes-a-Day" Book

THE CHRISTOPHERS
12 EAST 48TH STREET
NEW YORK, N.Y. 10017

ABOUT THE CHRISTOPHERS

We are an organization which uses the mass media: television, radio and the printed word to spread two basic ideas:

There's nobody like you.

You can make a difference.

The Christopher message is based on the Judeo-Christian concept of service to God and all humanity, and is addressed to people of all faiths and of no particular faith.

We believe...

● That you are a unique person.

● That your community, nation and world need what you have to give.

● That fault-finding has its place, but that constructive action is the best and most lasting response to the shortcomings of society.

● That each of us is called by God to become personally and actively involved in seeking solutions to the problems that confront us all.

● That each of us is entrusted with a job to do—one that has been given to no one else.

● That whoever and wherever we are, each of us has an opportunity to help shape the world we live in.

● That the basic approach is summed up in the words: "Be not overcome by evil, but overcome evil with good." (Romans 12:21)

The Christophers is a non-profit organization. We have no branches, no meetings, no dues. To meet our expenses, we depend on voluntary donations from people who believe that the individual can make a difference. We get no funding from church or government sources. All gifts are welcome—and deductible from taxable income.

The Christopher motto is an ancient Chinese proverb: "Better to light one candle than to curse the darkness."

To find out more about The Christophers—or to receive our News Notes free of charge seven times a year, write to:

The Christophers
Father John Catoir, Director
12 East 48th Street
New York, NY 10017
212-759-4050

YOU'RE REALLY SOMETHING

THE CHANGELING EAGLE

An American Indian legend tells about a brave who found an eagle's egg and put it into the nest of a prairie chicken. The eaglet hatched with the brood of chicks and grew up with them.

All his life, the changeling eagle—thinking he was a prairie chicken—did what the prairie chickens did.

He scratched in the dirt for seeds and insects to eat. He clucked and cackled. And he flew in a brief thrashing of wings and flurry of feathers no more than a few feet off the ground. After all, that's how prairie chickens were supposed to fly.

Years passed. And the changeling eagle grew very old. One day, he saw a magnificent bird far above him in the cloudless sky. Hanging with graceful majesty on the powerful wind currents, it soared with scarcely a beat of its strong golden wings.

"What a beautiful bird!" said the changeling eagle to his neighbor. "What is it?"

"That's an eagle. The chief of the birds," the neighbor clucked. "But don't give it a second thought. You could never be like him."

So the changeling eagle never gave it another thought. And it died thinking it was a prairie chicken.

● ● ●

It's all too easy to go through life thinking we're prairie chickens when we're really eagles. But doing so short-changes us and everyone else. Be what you are. Be all that you can be. Don't stay on the ground, when you have it in you to soar.

YOU HAVE WHAT IT TAKES

Psychologist William James described our condition very accurately:

"Most people live, whether physically, intellectually or morally, in a very restricted circle of their potential being. They make use of a very small portion of their possible consciousness, and of their soul's resources..."

Not Rebecca Johnson. Mrs. Johnson, 23, lives in Iowa City, Iowa. She decided to test her endurance by paddling a canoe down the Mississippi from Minnesota to the Gulf of Mexico—alone. Along the way, she met plenty of people who predicted she'd never make it.

"When I got to within 200 miles of New Orleans, people asked me where I was going and then they'd say, 'Lady, that's a long way.' I'd say, 'Not when you've already paddled 2,200 miles!'"

Was it worth the effort? Rebecca Johnson feels it was. "I've learned so much on this river," she says. "You learn about handling yourself. I think I could handle anything anybody wanted to throw at me now."

We don't have to paddle the length of the Mississippi to find out who we are. Sometimes, it takes a personal crisis or a severe physical, mental or emotional handicap. But not always.

Each day holds the chance to challenge ourselves a

little more, to ask a slightly tougher question, to go a little further out of our way to serve someone or explore something.

No one expects us to be foolhardy. But "playing it safe" is a sure way to cut down our chances of truly becoming all that we are. Dare to dare. You have what it takes.

> ## "Only that day dawns to which we are awake."
> ### —THOREAU

IF YOU WON'T WHO WILL?

Professor Abraham Maslow used to challenge his students with questions like: "Which of you is going to write the next novel?" and "Who is going to be a saint like Schweitzer?"

Confronted with such big ideas, the students would only blush, squirm and giggle. Then, the famed psychologist would assure them that he meant what he said.

"If not you, who will?" he demanded. We could each ask that question of ourselves. Blind chance didn't put us here. A loving God did, as part of His plan for creation. We are not given to know the total design of God's master plan.

But each day that dawns reveals a little of our portion of that plan. Each moment, God holds out a chance to be more, to achieve more. Each moment He gives us what we need to respond to that invitation. We have what it takes. Will we use it? If not us, who will?

DO YOU BELIEVE IN YOU?

The big first step in developing our full potential is to have faith in ourselves.

Kathy Peterson Rice believed in herself. And it got her through college. Under ordinary circumstances, she might never have even started. Mrs. Rice is dyslexic. She has a learning difficulty that makes it extremely difficult for her to read.

Her early years in school were frustrating. "I appeared to be a little slow and not too intelligent except I was quite good in math," she recalls. "But I was absolutely terrible with reading and spelling." At 13, she was diagnosed as dyslexic. She was given special help. Today she is a graduate engineer with a college record of straight A's.

What kept her from giving up? "Maybe stubbornness," she says. "I could never accept the idea that I absolutely could not do something. I think anybody can do almost anything if he sets his mind to it . . ."

Kathy Peterson Rice looks at a problem and sees a possibility. How about you?

**"Do not be afraid,
for I am with you."**

Isaiah

YOU'RE ON YOUR OWN!

No one can make us develop our potential—or do it for us. People can assist. They can show us how. But the choice is ours—to follow, to strike out on our own or to do nothing. That's what Robert Campbell, of Boston, Massachusetts, found out.

Mr. Campbell came from a family of writers and editors. So everyone assumed that he would follow his parents into journalism.

In college, he majored in English, although an aptitude test did uncover a certain flair for tactile and visual skills. He didn't take the evaluation too seriously. Just filed it away.

Mr. Campbell went on to journalism school. He worked with a large-circulation magazine for several years. But he never quite felt at home in his "inherited" profession. Then he remembered the test he had taken as a student.

At 26, Robert Campbell went back to school—to study architecture. Today, he is a working architect. "I feel good about it," he says. "I'll never get rich, but it's something I want to do."

He also pens a weekly article as architecture critic for *The Boston Globe*.

"It's impossible to waste time," he says of his years as a journalist. "There's nothing we've experienced that we can't incorporate into something we can do for the rest of our lives."

We are what we have been plus what we choose to become. What's your choice?

"It is common sense to take a method and try it. If it fails, admit it frankly and try another. But above all, try something."
—Franklin D. Roosevelt

START WHERE YOU ARE

"Evaluate your potential. Then expose yourself to the risk and reward of developing it," urges writer Sandra Ogle. It's good advice. If we don't make a start, we can't possibly get anywhere.

Thought, good advice, prayer, research—all go into choosing a course of action. But ultimately, the time to decide arrives—the moment for acting on the basis of what we have decided.

The process of making a start needn't be complex. It can begin right where you are—whenever you choose. It can be as simple as these suggestions sent by a Christopher friend in Kansas City. She tried to follow this basic program each day:

● Do something you *don't* want to do.

● Do something you *do* want to do.

● Be quiet for a few minutes for prayer, spiritual reading or meditation.

● Reach out in *some* way *every single* day to someone else.

"You know," she wrote, "it really works!" Try it. It can work for you, too.

> "Now is the favorable time."
> —St. Paul

MAKE A DIFFERENCE

Perhaps you're at a low point, wondering if you have any potential at all. If so, consider what happened to Ronald E. Gaddie of Ontario, California.

A little over 10 years ago, Mr. Gaddie was an out-of-work truck driver. Unable to drive because of a back injury, he was forced to go on welfare to support his wife and six children. To pass time following corrective surgery, he began raising earthworms.

Today, Ronald E. Gaddie is founder and president of his own business, North American Bait Farms, Inc. And he has produced an ecological bonus by demonstrating that worms can be used to recycle solid waste—at a profit. Their end product is a high-grade fertilizer worth 70¢ to $1 a pound.

His own city and several others have asked Mr. Gaddie to develop a worm-consumption program as part of their overall waste management system.

• • •

You may not be able to turn a hobby into a business idea. But you can:

• Make a list of the things you like to do, the things you want to do, and the things you have done successfully in the past. Include everything from "I had the lead in the third-grade play" to "I can bake good brownies."

- Discuss the list with one or two people whose opinion you respect and who have given you sound advice in the past. Objective feedback is always helpful.

- Pick one item that seems to be possible for you at this point in your life: You can afford it; you have the time; your family is behind you; it will not conflict with any of your current responsibilities.

- Do one constructive act toward making that possibility come true. Make the first phone call. Write the first letter. Buy the flour for the brownie sale. Whatever it is, take one concrete step toward achieving the goal you have chosen.

- Repeat the process each day, continuing to monitor the activity, to discuss it with your friends, to take any corrective action that seems to be necessary.

In a short period of time, you'll be amazed at where you find yourself.

Maybe you're at a low point. But you don't have to stay there.

With God's help and your own effort, you can make a move—and make a difference—today.

Eagle—or prairie chicken. It's up to you.

● ● ●

"Underachievers are not born, they are made." That's the view of Dr. Arthur Weider, a New York clinical psychologist.

He has spent years evaluating the potential of thousands of youngsters aged 14 to 21. And he has observed a lot of human potential not being utilized.

"We have to impart to underachievers the message that

there is hope to reverse the tide," he says. "Otherwise, as people mature, they modify their expectations—like shifting gears to a lower level of achievement."

Doctor Weider points out that, if people can find a goal in which they have a sincere interest and to which they can give themselves wholeheartedly, they may be amazed at what they can achieve.

"Often this goal has to be found by a trial and error system," he explains. "But when true commitment *is* found, it offers life's greatest satisfaction."

How we view ourselves plays a vital role in how we choose to spend our lives. So, don't sell yourself short. You're really something.

NEW YEAR'S RESOLUTIONS are almost as old as recorded history, claims Irene Keeney of the *Knickerbocker News*.

She cites ancient customs, including pagan man's extinguishing his fires and rekindling them and in some cultures the ceremony of paying all debts. "Wiping the slate clean" goes back to the old English custom of cleaning chimneys on New Year's Day.

Here are some of Ms. Keeney's hints on making and keeping resolutions:

- Don't set goals so high they can't be attained.
- Don't let resolutions mean "denial." If you achieve your goal, reward yourself.
- Remind yourself of resolutions by writing yourself little notes.
- If you fail, start over again. Don't give up.

Resolutions made on the first day of a fresh new year often wear thin. A formidable 365 days is a long time to "hang in there."

So why not concentrate on a goal just for today? With God's help, we can manage that.

> "I can do all things in Him who strengthens me." [PHILIPPIANS 4:13]

  In our weakness, Lord, may we find Your strength.

FELLOW POLICE OFFICERS call Robert Volpe, "Rembrandt." He combines what he loves—painting—with his job as a police detective.

The 34-year-old artist has been selling his paintings for 17 years. He has been a police officer for 13. His field is stolen and forged art works.

Detective Volpe, a native New Yorker, began painting as a child. When the time came to get a job, he joined the police force. His present assignment is unique in the nation.

With the eye of an artist, Robert Volpe knowledgeably moves in the art world and in the underworld. He is at home in pawn shops and in the homes of wealthy collectors, in museums and galleries.

When retirement comes, he plans to paint full time.

If you have the chance, guide youngsters to be true to what they know they are and can do. Encourage them to make the contribution that is uniquely theirs. They need courage—and encouragement—to be themselves.

"Guide me with Your counsel."

[PSALM 73:24]

May we be grateful, Father, for the gifts we have been given and use them constructively.

As a TV STAR, Will Hutchins earned more than ten times what he makes now. But he prefers being a clown for kids.

He's Patches the Clown—incongruous red ball of a nose on a sad face, tattered clothes. As part of a government-financed free theatre, he performs in schools and parks as well as in senior citizen centers.

The actor had lost his job as star of the Western, "Sugarfoot," when the series folded. Though unemployed for two years, he says he didn't miss the show. "It was like going to jail every day."

He got a job in a small circus. "I was scared at first," he says. "Luckily, I knew some magic tricks and soon had them laughing." In contrast to the many stars he knows who aren't happy, he is content with his new life. "I would rather see happiness on the faces of children."

Child or adult, each of us needs the release of laughter. To bring it to others is no small accomplishment. At a crucial time, it could change a life.

> "Make a joyful noise to the Lord . . . serve the Lord with gladness." [PSALM 100:1,2]

Surely you laughed with your friends, Jesus. Help us to lighten the hearts of those around us.

THERE EXISTS IN THE STATE of Washington an ancient Indian whaling village preserved in mud for about 300 years.

"Ozette is a Pompeii in mud instead of volcanic ash, an archeologist's dream," according to Richard Daugherty, anthropology professor. He was director of the digs at the Makah Indian village located 120 miles from Seattle.

"Whatever the reason," Professor Daugherty says, "a mudflow slammed into the village. Complete households were stopped in time." Materials used for daily life were discovered—mats, baskets, whaling harpoons, and combs (used for scratching not hair-combing).

Think for a minute. If you were "stopped in time" by a catastrophe, what story would the things in your life tell? What about our entire civilization?

What would archeologists of the future be able to say about us that is positive, favorable? Think about it.

"For what does it profit a man to gain the whole world and forfeit his life?"

[MARK 8:36]

Jesus, You said that what is in our hearts is our real treasure.

A NIGHTMARE STRUGGLE on broken ice made Canadian woodsmen Richard Carlson and John Halasz friends for life.

The men were driving snowmobiles over a frozen lake when Mr. Halasz's machine broke through. Heavy clothing and packsack pulled Mr. Halasz down, and he begged his partner to leave him and save himself.

Mr. Carlson drove his machine ashore, cut a birch sapling and crawled back over the crumbling ice. Dipping the pole under Mr. Halasz, now too numb to move, Mr. Carlson pried him onto the ice, dragged him to shore and built a fire to warm him.

Said Mr. Carlson afterward, "I figured that there was a very good chance I'd go in too, but I felt I had to keep his hopes up and try. You can't just let someone die."

"Greater love no man has than that a man lay down his life for his friend." Jesus said it and led the way. In small ways—and sometimes in large ones—we're called to follow.

> "By this we know love, that He laid down His life for us; and we ought to lay down our lives for the brethren." [1 JOHN 3:16]

℘ Jesus, make my love of neighbor strong.

RETIRED FIREMAN JOE TRICHILO of Syracuse, New York, received a surprise Christmas present—a visit from a boy he had saved from suffocation in 1961.

Bryan Wilcox was 17 months old when the fireman saved his life with mouth-to-mouth resuscitation. Sixteen years later, the teenager and his rescuer had a tearful reunion at the fireman's home.

Bryan and his family had lost track of the firefighter until recently, when they discovered his whereabouts and called to ask if they could visit him. The reunion "restored my faith in people" said Mr. Trichilo, who had been "sort of depressed" since a serious injury had incapacitated him.

"He thanked God for me," Joe Trichilo said, "he was glad for me... and that really got me."

Have you thanked the Lord lately for your friends? Prayed for them?

When St. Paul wrote to the Philippians, he said: "I thank my God in all my rememberance of you, always in every prayer of mine for you all, making my prayer with joy." [1:3]

      Thank you, Father, for my friends. May I never cease to appreciate them.

THIS YEAR WHEN PAUL PETZOLDT, 68, scaled Wyoming's rugged 13,766-foot Grand Teton Peak, he dedicated his climb "to the old folks at home."

Mr. Petzoldt, who has climbed the northwestern Wyoming peak hundreds of times since he was 16, is one of the few people who has done so in mid-winter. Every year since 1965, he has led a New Year's Day expedition.

"I get all sorts of letters from people in retirement homes who read about my climbs," he explained. "I suppose a lot of these senior citizens sort of project themselves onto me, and I love it. They look on me as the old guy who is still active."

There are lots of ways to stay active—even as we grow older and slow down physically. We can retain a lively interest in the day's events, in the news, in our families, in our neighbors.

We're never too old to retain a youthful heart and a desire to keep learning.

> "Walk as children of light . . . and try to learn what is pleasing to the Lord."
> [EPHESIANS 5:9,10]

℘ Fan the flame of curiosity in our hearts, Lord, so we'll want to find new horizons.

L ADY BUGS AND OTHER insects may go to work for University of Idaho scientists, if the research team can find taste treats delectable enough to lure the little bugs.

Dr. Guy Bishop, entomology professor, reports success in luring insects to potato fields with sprays combining honey and other sweets.

"We wanted to attract the helpful insects which prey on aphids and other insect pests," said Dr. Bishop. "Ladybird beetles and other beneficial insects seem to discover the presence of aphids because they are attracted to honeydew, the sweet excretion which aphids deposit on plant leaves," he explained.

Using bugs to control plant pests means poisonous insecticides don't have to be used. It's one way of cherishing God's good earth—and ours. There are others—some of which you can use in your daily life. Give it some thought.

> "The earth is the Lord's and the fullness thereof, the world and those who dwell therein." [PSALM 24:1]

ê Holy Spirit, may we cherish the beauty of creation.

NEITHER BLIZZARDS NOR AVALANCHES, grizzly bears nor timber wolves could deter Snowshoe Thompson from his regular delivery of the mail across the Sierras for a dozen years in the late 1800's. He traveled between Nevada and California making two to four roundtrips per month across the mountains regardless of the weather.

The mail carrier was born in Norway and brought to America as a child. He became a welcome figure to the miners and settlers as he made his rounds. His service was considered invaluable and so astonishing that now Snowshoe is being honored with a monument showing him on his heavy oak skis with a mail pack on his back.

Snowshoe Thompson saw a need and filled it—with dedication and, sometimes, heroism. He might have told you he was just doing a job. He was—but commitment and concern for others turned it into a life of service that is still remembered. Those attitudes can transform your life, too.

> "Every man shall give as he is able, according to the blessing of the Lord."
>
> [DEUTERONOMY 16:17]

ℰ Jesus, You went around doing good. Teach us to walk in Your steps.

ERE'S A MESSAGE from *Executives' Digest*:

"It costs nothing but creates much.

"It enriches those who receive without diminishing the wealth of those who give.

"It happens in a flash and the memory of it can last a lifetime.

"None are so rich that they can get along without it and none are so poor but are richer for a smile.

"It creates happiness in the home, fosters good will in a business and is the countersign of friends.

"It is rest to the weary, daylight to the discouraged and nature's best antidote for trouble.

"Yet it cannot be bought, begged, or stolen, for it is of no earthly good to anybody until it is given away.

"And if some person should be too tired to give you a smile, why not give one of your own?

"For nobody needs a smile so much as one who has none to give."

Smile more and watch what happens around you, and within you—whoever and wherever you are.

"Be of good cheer." [JOHN 16:33]

Remind us to bring Your joy to others, Lord.

BANJO, AN UNWANTED MONGREL, has changed the lives of the William Davis family of Dallas, Texas.

First of a new Canine Corps of "Hearing Ear Dogs," Banjo was trained by the American Humane Association to alert her deaf owners to water boiling, doorbells and telephones ringing, smoke alarms and other sounds.

The dog is also trained to be alert even to a crying infant. Trainer Agnes McGrath recorded baby cries and taught Banjo to go back and forth between her and the tape, hidden beneath a doll.

Mrs. Davis, who received Banjo, is deaf and the mother of a young baby. Furnished free by the AHA, the dog adjusted to her new duties within a month. The AHA now plans to set up eight new training sites.

The Hearing Ear Program, with headquarters at 5351 South Roslyn St., Englewood, Colorado 80110, is supported by voluntary contributions.

Can you use your ingenuity to make life easier for someone who is handicapped or ill?

"Having gifts that differ . . . let us use them."
[ROMANS 12:6]

May we use our gifts, Lord, to improve the quality of life for those around us.

A CHICAGO WOMAN BETWEEN JOBS became a "housesitter" because she has always wanted a gypsy way of life.

Jane Fitzgerald, a 37-year-old schoolteacher with a bachelor's degree in economics, moves into the houses of vacationing families to feed the pets, water the plants and keep burglars away. Her only fee is the price of a roof over her head, but she loves her new way of life.

She began it in 1976, when a friend's neighbors went to Europe and asked her to housesit for the summer.

"It wasn't as if I said, 'Well, now I'm going to become a housesitter,'" she explained, "but it was nice and I liked it."

Carrying all her possessions in a backpack, a Navy flight bag and a small metal case, Ms. Fitzgerald lives in a different house every few weeks. She says she loves the freedom and the lifestyle.

"Each to his own," we say of another's lifestyle. Do we mean it? Or do we judge? Jesus did not choose his friends according to appearances. He saw them as persons and each expanded in His friendship. He showed the way.

> "Render true judgments, show kindness and
> mercy, each to his brother."
>
> [ZECHARIAH 7:8]

Help me, Lord, to see others with Your eyes.

Tama, Japan's "city of tomorrow," has TV that talks back, teaches and delivers papers.

At the Tama New Town housing project in a Tokyo suburb, engineers linked 250 apartments by coaxial cable to give residents a sense of community. The experiment, a "living information system," is a joint project of Japan's telephone, electronics, newspaper and tele-communications systems.

Newspapers go directly to living rooms through a facsimile machine, which also provides sports and business papers, plus daily and local news geared for children. Pressing buttons brings to the TV screen news flashes, weather, even help in vacation planning. Students and teachers communicate directly by audio-visual hookup for primary math and English classes.

Electronic wizardry like that in Tama, Japan, may make your head spin. But remember: It can be a great boon to humankind. Work and pray for a technology that puts people first. We can achieve it if we want to.

"Unless the Lord builds the house, those who build it labor in vain."   [PSALM 127:1]

ಶಿ Holy Spirit, guide scientists and engineers in building tomorrow's world.

YES, YOUNG PEOPLE ARE RELIABLE, willing workers when given the chance. And Y.E.S.—Youth Employment Service—tries to give them just that—an opportunity to earn money and get work experience.

The Pleasantville, New York, program matches employers and kids. Jobs range from construction site cleanup work to babysitting. Y.E.S. operates year round using federal funds as well as contributions from area businesses and communities.

According to the program directors, one key to its success is its local base. Businesses and homeowners seem inclined to hire the youngsters because they know they're local residents.

We often look to Big Government, Big Business (and "Big Money") to solve our problems for us. But a lot of needs can be dealt with right where you are. Changing your world often starts with changing your home town, even your block, for the better.

"Happy are we if we exercise justice and constantly practice virtue." [PSALM 106:3]

Father, spur us to seek solutions to what needs doing.

Two New York subway motormen who were neighbors weren't thinking about blazing a trail in race relations back in 1942. But that's what they did.

The Hollis Discussion Club, which just celebrated its 35th anniversary, began when Herb Coddington, a black man, and Russell Marks, a white man, started weekly evenings of neighborhood debate.

There's no subject, they say, that they haven't covered in their 800 meetings—some with speakers.

"It's hard to believe now," says Mr. Coddington, "but in those days if a black man and a white man walked down the street together people would stare at them."

The neighborhood has since been quietly integrated. And the pioneer group? "It's like an extended family," says Herb Coddington's son, Robert.

Doing things together—work, study or play—creates a bond. Stressing what we share can make our own community more of a family.

> "Let us consider how to stir up one another to love and good works." [HEBREWS 10:24]

ℰℰ Help me, Father, to take that first step in knowing those who are different from me.

THE AIR AMERICANS BREATHE was 33 percent cleaner in 1974 than it was in 1970, according to the U.S. Environmental Protection Agency.

Among findings of the agency are these facts:

● Carbon monoxide levels dropped 70-81 percent at 102 sites in 24 states.

● Concentrations of airborne sulfur dioxide have decreased in 545 urban areas by 30 percent.

● Populations exposed to air unduly high in "total suspended particulates" dropped from 73 million to 49 million.

● Despite all the above improvements, some 30 percent of the United States population still live in areas where the particulate level is unacceptable.

In the effort to clean up the air we breathe, even major efforts will take years to succeed.

It is almost a rule of life that any worthwhile endeavor takes a lot of patience, energy and time.

Knowing it won't be easy is no reason for refusing to make the effort.

> "'Take courage, all you people of the Land,' says the Lord; 'work, for I am with you.'"
> [HAGGAI 2:4]

℮ð   Sharpen our sense of purpose, Lord, and keep us from discouragement.

A TALENT FOR COOKING and menu planning hasn't kept Atlanta's Judy Stokes home in her kitchen. Mrs. Stokes, 36, is dietary consultant to 75 nursing homes and hospitals. She is also nutrition consultant to the Georgia penal system.

Mrs. Stokes has done graduate work in home economics, experimental foods and dietetics institutional management, and is president of her own company. With a staff of six registered dieticians, she gives help with menu-planning, special dietary needs, Medicare regulations and drug-food interactions.

After serious riots, she did a nutritional analysis for Oklahoma State Prison, redesigning menus for proper nutrition, variety and taste. "It's very challenging, very exhausting," she says of her work. "I love it."

Judy Stokes took her love for cooking and turned it into a life's work that makes her happy and enriches hundreds of other people.

What do you love to do? Maybe a little thought and effort will serve up a recipe for your life.

"Only let your manner of life be worthy of the Gospel of Christ."   [PHILIPPIANS 1:27]

ₑ₵ Holy Spirit, teach us to live creatively.

A PROMINENT PSYCHOLOGIST and educator says that the wicked witch and the big, bad wolf are just what children need.

Tales of fantasy, says Bruno Bettelheim, professor at the University of Chicago, mirror the anxieties of childhood and help children adjust to them. His book, *The Uses of Enchantment: The Meaning and Importance of Fairy Tales,* explains his theory.

The Frog Prince and Beauty's Beast, which Dr. Bettelheim claims are symbols of something negative in sex, are transformed through love.

Many stories begin with the death of a parent—a major childhood fear. But they resolve the problem and on a subconscious level reassure the child that his or her anxieties and conflicts can be resolved, too.

"Without such fantasies," says Dr. Bettelheim, ". . . the child remains helpless with his worst anxieties."

Tales of fantasy were told long before the printed, or even the written word. Even older in human history is love, the greatest comforter of all.

> "This is the message which you have heard from the beginning, that we should love one another." [1 JOHN 3:11]

> ᏲᏋ May we be able, Lord, to give children assurance that they are loved.

I N CITIES WHICH ENJOY excellent medical care, there can be serious pockets of medical poverty.

A study of the city's 18,137 physicians by New York's Department of Health revealed a startling fact. While richer neighborhoods boasted as many as 42 doctors for every 1,000 people, slum areas had as few as one doctor for 22,000.

One Bronx neighborhood of 10,000 people had no doctor at all, and the survey showed dozens of poor districts with virtually no medical care within miles.

According to New York City Health Commissioner Dr. Pascal Imperato, health problems in the slum areas are compounded by the inability of residents to travel to the doctors in affluent neighborhoods.

What is the situation in your city? If you are aware of a dearth of available physicians in any one area, there may be something you can do.

For one thing, you could make your voice heard in an effort to raise the level of health care in the community.

"Those who are well have no need of a physician, but those who are sick." [MARK 2:17]

ᵉᶅ Lord, bless those seeking to continue Your healing ministry.

SIX YEARS OF BLINDNESS ENDED suddenly for Connie Green of Dayton, Ohio, when she looked up from dinner and saw her family.

A head injury had blinded her at age 27. Then, unaccountably, her sight began returning while she was at a friend's wedding. She began to make out images. Later that day, at dinner, she saw her family clearly.

Doctors, mystified by the recovery, warned Mrs. Green that it could vanish as quickly as it came. But she has few fears. Of her newly found sight she says:

"If I lose it again, I will have no regrets. I've learned to love people more. I've learned to take time to love people more. Most people don't take that time."

Why is it that most of us are slow to learn what is really important—to show our care for others and to accept it in return? It shouldn't take a tragedy to make us realize the value of today.

"Ah, this is the day we longed for; now we have it!" [LAMENTATIONS 2:17]

❧ Give us wisdom, Lord, to pick out the important in the midst of the ordinary.

PROBLEM YOUNGSTERS TUTOR younger pupils in several New York schools.

In a pilot project designed to help sixth graders by encouraging them to help other children, the tutors are selected because they are disruptive, truant or have other behavior problems. Results are surprisingly encouraging. Both "teachers" and their younger charges are making steady gains in reading ability.

After 400 pupils were successfully involved in one program, in District 7 of the Bronx, the plan is being tested in Albany, New York, and Stamford and Hartford, Connecticut.

Explained one tutor, describing her instruction of a third grader, "It helps me read better and understand. I have to go over it before I can help him."

It's true. It often "takes one to know one"—and to help one, whatever "one" may be. In this case, it's students helping students. In your life, it may be something else. An ideal starting point may be just waiting for you to find it.

> "Learn where there is wisdom, where there is strength, where there is understanding."
> [BARUCH 3:14]

Father, show us ways to be instruments of Your love.

A YOUNG WOMAN WROTE this letter to Ann Landers. "I've read a lot lately about how ungrateful kids are. I wonder if some of the parents who read your column will see themselves in a little different light after they have answered these questions:

• When was the last time you spent an hour with your child—doing what he wanted?

• When was the last time you said to your child, 'You did a great job. I'm proud of you!'?

• When did you last say, 'Let's talk about anything you want to talk about. I'll listen and answer all your questions if I can'?

• When was the last time you said, 'I'm sorry,' or 'I made a mistake'?

• How long has it been since you said, 'I trust you. I know you have good judgment and will do the right thing'?

I'm a 16-year-old girl and I've never heard one of these statements from either of my parents...

Not Sour, Just Sad"

"A gentle tongue is a tree of life, but perverseness in it breaks the spirit." [PROVERBS 15:4]

ᏋᏋ   Help us, Father, to be more aware of what our children need from us.

JOURNALISTS IN BONN, West Germany, recently enjoyed a banquet of arctic cod, cream of krill soup, Chinese grass fish, algae and soybean salad.

Demonstrating little-used foods which can combat world starvation, the menu was the result of projects for which the West German Ministry of Research and Technology has spent about $50 million since 1970.

Some 400 million people are starving, Research Minister Hans Matthoefer told the luncheon guests. Another 400 million are undernourished. But, said Mr. Matthoefer, protein can be produced from fish from the depths of the Atlantic and Antarctic, from methane, methanol, paraffin, cellulose, lignite and sewage.

Mass production of algae, exotic plants, fish, mussels, oysters and shrimps is also being developed.

We can feed a hungry world. The obstacle is not lack of nourishing food. It's lack of will, political rivalries and inadequate distribution mechanisms.

Pray, work and give for the day when no one will have to sit down at an empty dinner table.

"Give them something to eat."
[MATTHEW 14:16]

⌘ Jesus, You fed the hungry. Show us how to do the same.

SUSAN SYGALL, 18, planned a career in recreation. She hoped to work with disabled persons. She went to Colorado for studies. Four days after she arrived, a car accident left her paralyzed from the legs down.

Instead of changing her plans, she became more deeply involved in the recreation field. Eventually, with a friend, Diane Schechter, she began the Berkeley Outreach Recreation Program in California.

One class offers self-defense for the physically handicapped. Disabled persons learn they don't have to be helpless if attacked. They discover how wheelchairs, canes and crutches can become self-defense tools.

Susan Sygall found a way to build a life's ambition around a crippling accident. We all have weaknesses, setbacks, reversals. It's not so much what happens to us as what we do with it that spells success or failure in a life.

> "The Lord stood by me and gave me strength."
> [2 TIMOTHY 4:17]

℘ Father, never let us forget that in our weakness is Your strength.

FOR INDIAN ARTIST Chanan Singh, bigger is definitely not better. Mr. Singh has painted 400 pictures in the past 30 years—on grains of rice!

A map draftsman for the Indian government, the 53-year-old painter probably produces the world's smallest pictures. He has applied to the Guinness Book of Records for recognition. Among his works are portraits of President Carter, Queen Elizabeth II and Canada's Prime Minister Pierre Trudeau.

"People are doing bigger and bigger things, and I say let us go smaller and smaller," he says. "Utilize space. Do maximum work given minimum space."

Carrying his tiny paintings in glass tubes, Mr. Singh has taken them on a world tour to exhibit.

The artist is right—bigger doesn't always mean better. Do you live a life of "more," "new," "big," "costly?"

Consider scaling down your lifestyle. You just may find that little things do mean a lot.

> "Well done, good and faithful servant! You have been faithful over a little, I will set you over much." [MATTHEW 25:21]

ಜ್ Father, give us appreciation of life's small joys.

IN FRANCE, A POST OFFICE is a lot more than a place to mail packages and letters.

In a French post office, you can buy life insurance, annuities and telegrams; take out loans; open savings accounts; make overseas phone calls; and even buy treasury bonds and mutual funds.

The French post office sends almost anything anywhere. It even transmits long verbal messages to other post offices where they are committed to writing and delivered.

To accomplish all this, 430,000 highly trained and efficient employees work for the Ministry of Post, Telegraph and Telephone. Their slogan—"Yours Day by Day"—has the letter "o" shown as a heart.

When it comes to delivering services to people, each of us can function as a mini-post office. We do well when we are efficient, but we do our best when we put "heart" into our delivery system.

God sends some of His blessings to the world through you and me. How efficient and wholehearted are we?

> "Whatever good the Lord will do to us, the same will we do to you." [NUMBERS 10:32]

  Help us to care about the people in our lives, Lord, so that we may do more for them—and do it better.

"I WAS SICK AND YOU VISITED ME..."

THROUGH DR. MEAD BAILEY's chaplain's aide program, gravely ill patients at New York's Bellevue Hospital gain new vision and courage.

Thirty aides with intensive six-week training work with troubled patients, helping them talk about anger, fear and feelings of hopelessness.

"Because we're not wearing a white collar like the chaplains," says volunteer Joanne Teitelbaum, "we have an advantage." The aides do not preach, but help patients regain a sense of dignity and control over their lives.

Aides are needed each fall to begin training sessions, says volunteer director Louise Davidson. "We need volunteers who are warm and supportive and outgoing, who can listen to patients."

Have you ever thought of volunteer work in a hospital, a nursing home, with youngsters or shut-ins? If you have the time and the interest, consider it. Someone needs what you have to give. Are you willing to give it?

"Do not neglect to do good and to share what you have."   [HEBREWS 13:16]

℮ Jesus, inspire us to reach out to the suffering and lonely, as you did.

Two WOMEN IN WASHINGTON, D.C., love their work. They're paperhangers—not decorators, they insist—paperhangers.

Barbara Gale, whose husband is director of recruiting for the Peace Corps, has teamed up with Helen Whittemore, wife of the poet in residence at the Library of Congress.

While their friends are involved with ceramics, yoga or school, Mrs. Gale and Mrs. Whittemore go off to work with their overalls and buckets of paste. They give advice on selection of papers but prefer to specialize in hanging it.

"It's a kind of therapy," says Barbara Gale. They find it gives "instant satisfaction," and both women take pride in the skill with which they do it.

Is there a source of satisfaction, a reason for legitimate self-esteem, in your life? It needn't be a job—though it may be. Look for a way of self-expression. You'll enrich your own life... and maybe a couple of others.

> "Decide on a matter, and it will be established
> for you, and light will shine on your ways."
> [JOB 22:28]

Father, You are Creator of all. Help us to be more creative.

EMPLOYEES DON'T ALWAYS REALIZE that good business requires that a company know when it's in the wrong and do something about it. *Executives' Digest* suggests this way of handling irate customers:

1. Welcome the complaint; don't resent it.

2. Empathize. Acknowledge that you would feel the same if it had happened to you.

3. Display initiative. Show some interest and, in the customer's presence, take some constructive action.

4. Indicate the next steps. Describe what you will do and approximately how long it will take.

5. Try to compensate. Try to provide some extra service or courtesy in view of the loss suffered.

6. Follow up. Show that the company cares. Set a deadline for the follow-up and contact the customer before he or she contacts you.

What it really boils down to is caring enough about another to show concern and try to help. Jesus phrased it: "Love your neighbor as yourself." [ROMANS 13:9]

    Lord, help us to see the other person's point of view.

IN THE TRAGEDY OF DIVORCE, there are legal and personal aids for the couple and their children. But what about the grandparents?

In many cases, a parent cuts ties with the other family so that children and one set of grandparents never see each other. For others, visits are few.

Grandparents who find themselves left out are now turning to professionals, often for the first time in their lives. "These are kind of daring, brave people we're seeing," says a family counselor. "They're in a great deal of pain."

"It's like a death to both parties," says a Michigan woman, Louella Davison, "the grandparents and the grandchildren." She decided to start Grandparents Anonymous "when I was feeling real blue about my own situation." The group has gathered 5,000 signatures in support of legislation for visitation rights.

Such pain is a reminder of how our lives are intertwined. But hope exists—love multiplies itself just as surely as pain. Put more love in your life.

"None of us lives to himself, and none of us dies to himself." [ROMANS 14:7]

ẽ᷏ Lord, make us instruments of Your love.

An OLD, LARGE RED BRICK building, the abandoned Public School No. 1 in Long Island City, New York, has been transformed into a place for experimental artists to create and display their work.

"What we're about is helping fine artists to produce good art," said Alanna Heiss, director at the Institute of Art and Urban Resources. The institute is helping artists find suitable places to work in buildings that might otherwise stay empty. By refurbishing the school, which was to have been wrecked, the artists were able to create a community. "There's a general feeling of community, but if you want to be alone you can," said sculptor Robert Grosvenor.

Ours has been called the "throw-away society." But—given the ecological crunch point we are at—things can't go on that way much longer. Can you recycle, mend, refurbish or repair? A little thought might show where to begin.

"All things are from God."
[1 CORINTHIANS 11:12]

℘ Holy Spirit, make us resourceful in using our resources.

Louise Daniel Hutchinson, a research director in Washington, D.C., has created an exhibit chronicling the achievements of over 150 black women whose exploits are generally omitted from history books.

A major goal of the exhibit is to portray these women in their varied roles as writers, educators and inventors. Ms. Hutchinson knew one such woman, Mary McLeod Bethune, a member of Franklin D. Roosevelt's "Black Cabinet." "She was a woman of great faith," Ms. Hutchinson recalls. "She thought that anything she wanted— and there never was anything she wanted for herself— God would make possible."

Skill, faith and dedication know no race, sex, creed or color. That's why it's such a tragic, senseless mistake to set up boundaries that exclude people. In the long run, the ones who do the excluding are the big losers.

> "Hold fast what is good, abstain from every form of evil."   [1 THESSALONIANS 5:21]

Holy Spirit, remind us that we are all God's children.

WHAT WOULD LIFE be like for you if you were one of the world's poorest people in the world's poorest countries? This profile was drawn by the Organization for Economic Cooperation and Development:

● You're an illiterate farmer, working mountainous, desert, grassland or salt-pan terrain.

● You live at least 20 miles from a road, hundreds of miles from a seaport.

● You live even farther from any health service or school.

● If you should wish to leave your rural subsistence, you cannot. There are no industries to hire you.

● Your home is probably in southern Africa or Southeast Asia.

World poverty isn't really an "us—them" situation. The hungry farmer in Chad, the cold shepherd in Afghanistan, all God's poor are our brothers and sisters. In our abundance is their hope. Find ways to reach them.

> "Open wide your hand to your brother, to the needy and to the poor, in the land."
> [DEUTERONOMY 15:11]

eĉ   Father, may we not hold back when it is within our power to help.

Deaf university student John Pitts couldn't talk with fellow-freshmen at Michigan State University, so he designed a t-shirt with the alphabet in sign language on it.

Inscribed "Let's Talk," the ingenious method will help people communicate with those who are deaf, says Mr. Pitts, who hopes to mass-produce the design on t-shirts and beach towels.

The son of deaf parents, John Pitts took up accounting at MSU, and became frustrated by the difficulty he had in communicating with other students.

"Then I reasoned for five weeks how I could talk with people and I decided to make the shirt," he said through a sign language interpreter. "I hope my t-shirt will help the whole situation with deaf people."

It isn't only the deaf who have difficulties in communication. All of us experience the frustration and the confusion that can result from not being able "to get through to" another person.

How much clarity and good will could come from just trying to make our own "signals" more understandable!

"Give me understanding." [PSALM 119:34]

ﷺ Help us, Jesus, to communicate with each other in love.

Stewart B. McKinney received a $3,100 pay raise but declined to take it, deciding to give it away instead.

When Connecticut representative McKinney was in his third term, Congress voted for the raise in the $45,600 annual salary of its members.

Mr. McKinney refused to take it, however, because of a belief that such raises shouldn't be granted in the same session in which they are approved.

He decided to give his raise to three districts in his area needing the extra financial help, Bridgeport, Stamford and Norwalk, that is, $1,033 each.

Few of us can afford to refuse a pay raise. It's not so easy to recognize that neither can we afford to ignore our principles.

The world will get no better unless those who care enough will act according to the inner voice which tells them what is right to do.

"Walk in the way of righteousness, in the paths of justice." [PROVERBS 8:20]

ǝ Father, help me to be true to my principles.

THE MIRACLE OF A BUTTERFLY'S BIRTH is the gift Arlene Hoffman has given to her ad agency co-workers.

Ms. Hoffman, vice-president of New York ad agency Burson-Marsteller Company, had raised Monarch butterfly caterpillars at home as a hobby. She gathers them as eggs on milkwood plants.

"It's such a thrilling experience," says Ms. Hoffman, "I decided to share it." Now she keeps milkwood plants with their caterpillar tenants in her office through the five-week growth cycle of caterpillar to chrysalis to butterfly.

How does the office staff like it? Says Ms. Miller: "Everybody, from the top management all the way down, is absolutely enthralled by it. This is more than birth, this is true magic—a metamorphosis. You go to sleep for a certain amount of time and you wake up and you can fly."

When we awaken the awareness and sense of wonder we had as children, we can experience and share the delight of the miracles that have been around us all along.

"For behold, I create new heavens and a new earth."   [ISAIAH 65:17]

ec   Father, may we live with joy in the gifts You have provided.

ARE YOU SHY? If so, you're not alone. Many people consider shyness a serious personal problem.

Professor Philip Zimbardo of Stanford University interviewed 2,000 students. Forty-two percent considered themselves shy.

"Our culture emphasizes individuality," he said, "individual achievement and success. Once you have a concept of success, you have to have another of failure. So you're always concerned about failure."

Professor Zimbardo cites, by contrast, Chinese society, in which shyness appears to be nearly non-existent. He attributes this to the Chinese emphasis on group success rather than individual achievement.

Social awkwardness, hesitancy to speak, reluctance to be touched or to look another in the eye all can be signs of shyness.

The most direct way to overcome shyness is also the hardest. It involves doing what we fear to do. Happily, if we try, we'll discover "the sky won't fall in."

> "Fear not, for I am with you, be not dismayed, for I am your God; I will strengthen you, I will help you." [ISAIAH 41:10]

🙏 Increase our confidence in ourselves, Holy Spirit, and our trust in You.

W RITING MAY DATE back 10,000 years, according to new evidence found by Denise Schmandt-Besserat of Texas.

Mrs. Schmandt-Besserat, assistant director of the University of Texas Center for Middle Eastern Studies, believes that writing grew as a way to symbolize small tokens used in trade.

Around 3,500 B.C., she says, the tokens appeared in clay envelopes called bullae, used by traders. Goods were consigned to a middle man with a bulla containing the number of tokens equivalent to the shipment, she writes. Then, bullae appeared with signs on the surface representing the tokens inside.

"We thought that writing came out of nowhere," says Mrs. Schmandt-Besserat, "but this puts writing in the perspective of a recording system that existed all along."

Nothing comes out of nowhere. Like most other inventions, writing grew out of a real human need. Want to be creative? Look for a problem in need of a solution and get going. The outcome may surprise you.

> "I considered these things inwardly and thought upon them in my mind."
>
> [WISDOM 8:17]

෧ Holy Spirit, free our minds to be more creative.

SOME 200 NEW YORK PRISONERS are paying their debt to society by creating beauty in the state's forests.

In a program growing in popularity, five state correction department camps house young men 16 to 25 years old who work with the Department of Environmental Conservation. Cleaning and improving streambeds, building horse and snow mobile trails are some of the projects that get youths into the open air and out of a prison atmosphere.

"They gain no time off from being here," says camp director Jim Wilmington. The living conditions and routine are spartan. But volunteers among minimum security prisoners are plentiful.

Adds forester Frank Bulsiewicz, "I know we are doing as much for the human resource as we are for wildlife. All of them learn the values of the outdoor."

Our penal system can be administered creatively—as this program shows. The big question is, are we, the citizens, making our voices heard in support of such innovation?

> "Remember those who are in prison, as though in prison with them."
>
> [HEBREWS 13:3]

ε₂ Holy Spirit, guide persons of high ideals into prison work.

FIVE EXCUSES FOR NOT WORKING to change the world were listed by the *Royal Bank of Canada Monthly Letter*. They go hand in hand with complacency and failure:

"I am too young." All too soon time denies this excuse. Learning capacity peaks before age 25.

"I have no time." Just giving up the comic pages in two newspapers adds 20 minutes of study time daily. Better use of time means choosing among activities.

"It is too dull." Some things may be dull. But somewhere there is a path leading to success.

"It is too hard." Henry Drummond said, "Unless a man undertakes more than he can possibly do, he will never do all that he can do."

"I am too old." History shows that one is never too old to do something worthwhile. Instead of something planned in youth, it may be an achievement growing out of years of life experience.

Making excuses as to why we can't do things can rob us of zest for living. The Lord has given abilities to each of us! Let us use them.

> "Go, do all that is in your heart; for the Lord is with you." [2 SAMUEL 7:3]

ɛՖ Prompt us, Holy Spirit, to do our part to make the world a better place.

Any of Geraldine Naunheim's younger grandchildren can pick up the doll she invented and say, "That's me." The doll's face is an unbreakable acrylic mirror.

"Kids are fascinated with mirrors," says Mrs. Naunheim, a St. Louis resident. In 1970, she made the first doll for her granddaughter, Jennifer, then 5.

Graphic Resources, a firm which designs educational aids, heard about the Me Doll and is paying the 75-year-old grandmother a royalty for marketing it. With a teacher's guide and a recording, it is used for retarded children and developmentally delayed infants.

"I read so much about people not knowing who they are," says Mrs. Naunheim. "I hope this doll helps kids develop a strong concept of themselves."

Children see themselves reflected, too, in the responses of adults to what they say and do. We make them feel worthwhile when we show awareness of them as persons in our praise, our corrections, our listening.

"Do unto others" applies to all ages.

"Above all hold unfailing your love for one another."　　　　　　　　[1 PETER 4:8]

❧　Help me, Jesus, to see in each person his or her dignity as a child of God.

An "ALMOST-FREE REPAIR SHOP" is a neighborhood project on New York's Lower East Side.

The program, begun 30 years ago by the Henry Street Settlement, brings together volunteers and paid professionals to repair household items. In a noisy but brightly painted basement, men watch or work with TV and radio repairmen, cobblers repair shoes for the cost of materials, and sewing instructors help housewives alter or mend clothing. Furniture is stripped and refinished, clocks are repaired and owners have the chance to learn a valuable trade.

"When I came here I didn't know much," says one woman. "I made these two dresses for $4.05. You can forget everything outside—all your problems—when you come here."

A lot of us could "make do" with what we have if we knew how to fix things. We can promote conservation and fight inflation by learning a skill to save money and materials.

"I, wisdom, dwell in prudence."

[PROVERBS 8:12]

ê   Lead us to be more economy-minded, Lord, so we may respect Your creation.

THE MORE PROMINENT the individual, the more intriguing become the little things about him or her.

On a recent February 12th, Daniel Boorstin, Librarian of Congress, opened for the first time a small box that had belonged to Mary Lincoln, the President's granddaughter. It contained the contents of Lincoln's pockets on the night he was assassinated.

Before the eyes of library officials and journalists, he removed the items one by one: Two pairs of eyeglasses, a penknife, a watch fob, a cuff link with the initial "L," a handkerchief with "A. Lincoln" embroidered in red, and a wallet containing a $5 bill and nine newspaper clippings.

The clippings, all favorable, included a letter to newspaperman Horace Greeley, praising Lincoln's singleness of purpose and unfaltering patriotism.

Somehow it's comforting to have evidence that the great man valued praise—just like the rest of us. So do the people with whom you live and work. Try to give it.

> "If there is any excellence, if there is anything worthy of praise, think about these things."
> [PHILIPPIANS 4:8]

ॐ   Help us, Lord, to realize how alike we all are in our basic needs.

A LOAN FROM THE BANK at which she had embezzled funds gave an Albany, New York, teenager a second chance in life.

When the 19-year-old girl pleaded guilty to taking $2,150 from the First National Bank of Scotia, her attorney pointed out that she was the oldest of seven children and had worked while attending high school. He noted that her employers felt she was a "model employee" and said she had been "caught in a web of circumstances" she will "regret the rest of her life."

Then, in a surprise move, the bank which was the teenager's former employer offered to loan her the money to be repaid by $61 monthly for four years.

Saying that he found the unusual arrangement acceptable in the girl's case, United States District Court Judge James Foley placed her on two years' probation.

Loaning an embezzler the money to make restitution for her crime is an outstanding instance of "going the extra mile." In ways unique to our circumstances, it's a divine injunction each of us can heed.

> "Forgive, if you have anything against anyone; so that your Father also who is in heaven may forgive you your trespasses."
>
> [MARK 11:26]

ɛↄ Lord, remind us that "it is in pardoning that we are pardoned."

M ERYL DUNSMORE'S SECRET ADMIRER has sent her a Valentine each year since 1928, when the Toronto woman was 16.

For 50 years, Mrs. Dunsmore has received the cards, each with a brief declaration of love, but no name. Through the Depression, two marriages, a world war and six changes of address, the cards have kept coming, airmailed from such exotic places as Thailand, Barcelona, Johannesburg, Tokyo, Germany and the Caribbean. The messages of love have come in a dozen different languages.

Mrs. Dunsmore has no idea who is sending them. Her husband, who is equally mystified, says he's just as thrilled as she is.

Love is always a balm and always welcome. It can ease wounds, heal slights, resolve arguments. But it isn't always easy. It means opening ourselves to others—each day there are opportunities.

Are we willing to love?

"Let all we do be done in love."
[1 CORINTHIANS 16:14]

&c   Lord, help me to be alert to people in need.

IN A UNIQUE PROGRAMMING venture, a Hartford, Connecticut, affiliate of CBS-TV turned the tables and listened to its audience.

WFSB pre-empted its prime-time broadcasting for three and a half hours one night to give members of the audience and home viewers a chance to air their needs and interests. The show, "Nobody Ever Asked Me," according to manager Daniel Gold, will help the station select its programs and news stories.

Topics ranged from concern with unemployment and the economy to complaints that the station never covered news of what "good children" in the community were doing.

A welfare mother took her moment before the camera to say that "Lots of us can't afford to eat decent because we can't afford food stamps."

Despite competition from sports and entertainment programs, WFSB led all other TV stations in the area in viewer ratings for the full three and a half hours.

Listening has its rewards for individuals, too. To listen is to learn, perhaps to know someone better.

> "Listen to advice and accept instruction that you may gain wisdom for the future."
> [PROVERBS 19:20]

❧ May we hear Your voice, Lord, in the events of our lives, in our relationships with others.

ENGLISH SCIENTISTS HAVE DEVELOPED an organism which is half plant and half animal, apparently breaking the "kingdom barrier" successfully for the first time.

It is felt that one of the more exciting aspects of this breakthrough is the possibility of growing plant-animal hybrid tissue on a large scale as food. According to researchers, this might, for example, lead to plants that have the taste and nutrition of beef.

These hybrids could be particularly useful since they may combine the attractive texture and nutritional value of animal proteins with the ability of plants to grow almost anywhere.

The persistence of those doing this research could one day contribute to controlling, even eliminating the problem of world hunger.

But we can't wait for miracles of science. We need the miracle of caring people right now—people who care enough to be aware of hunger in their communities and elsewhere and to do something about it.

"What then shall we do? . . . He who has two coats, let him share with him who has none and he who has food, let him do likewise."

[LUKE 3:10,11]

Help us to think of the pain of hunger, Father, and to stir ourselves out of apathy.

Dr. Patricia Jakubowski, of the University of Missouri, cites 10 human rights:

- Right to refuse requests without having to feel guilty or selfish.
- Right to feel and express appropriate anger.
- Right to feel and express a healthy competitiveness and achievement drive.
- Right to strive for self-actualization through whatever ethical channels are natural to one.
- Right to use one's judgment in deciding which needs are the most important for one to meet.
- Right to make mistakes.
- Right to have one's opinions given the same respect that other people's opinions are given.
- Right to be treated as a capable human adult and not to be patronized.
- Right to have one's needs be as important as those of others.
- Right to be independent.

Do you claim—and grant—those rights?

> "God did not give us a spirit of timidity but a spirit of power and love and self-control."
>
> [2 TIMOTHY 1:7]

Help me to remember, Lord, that I am to love others as I love myself—and to start loving myself.

T WENTY-THREE-YEAR-OLD DEIRDRE WHITEHEAD has become a skilled ivory carver. Hired as a cafeteria worker, she spent her spare time watching scrimshaw artists at the Alaskan Silver and Ivory Company in Bellingham, Washington. Fascinated, she tried it herself.

"It was so frustrating," she recalls. "You have to have a firm but delicate touch. But it was comforting to know that if I made a mistake, I could grind it off and begin again."

Now an accomplished carver, Deirdre uses a magnifying optic visor, ultra-sharp carving tools and india ink to produce art objects—some taking up to two weeks to complete.

"I have learned that by working hard I can do anything," she says. "Right now I really want to be a terrific scrimshander."

Young people often have a hard time putting direction in their lives. Learning to do one thing well is a good start. Encourage them.

"We exhorted each one of you and encouraged you and charged you to lead a life worthy of God."   [1 THESSALONIANS 2:11]

May we encourage young people, Lord, to use the talent You have given them.

CLAUDIO GONZALEZ OF CHILE wrote this to the Nobel Prize-winning organization, Amnesty International:

"...I was one of those people you worked for in such a dignified and intense way so that the steel walls of the concentration camps would open up and so that I would be able to exercise the inalienable right of every human being to think and to walk in freedom...I ask you to accept my deepest gratitude..."

Amnesty International dates back to 1961 when a British newspaper article entitled "The Forgotten Prisoner" stirred some concerned people to action.

It is now worldwide with nearly 100,000 members in 33 countries. It has aided over 9,000 men and women who were prisoners of conscience, i.e. "those imprisoned anywhere for their political or religious beliefs, color or ethnic origin, who have neither used nor advocated violence."

One man wrote an article. A handful of people responded. And 9,000 people are free. A small lever can move so much.

"Those who lead the many to justice shall be like the stars forever." [DANIEL 12:3]

Help us to understand, Lord, that if we care enough we can build Your Kingdom on earth.

Every Saturday morning in the 50's and 60's, Kirby Grant, star of "Sky King," a popular TV show, used to rescue a niece and nephew from some peril.

Today at 65, Mr. Grant is still rescuing kids. These are unwanted youngsters, ranging in age from 9 to 16, who might otherwise be institutionalized. "Any day, across the country," he says, "you can find 350,000 or more youngsters in jails, or places like jails."

He heads the non-profit Sky King Youth Ranches of America, Inc. With donations, he and his wife set up their first "youth ranch" in Winter Park, Florida, in 1976, a five-bedroom home for nine girls, with an adult couple as houseparents. They have since opened another for boys.

"The idea," says Kirby Grant, "is for youngsters to live as part of a family unit until they are ready to go off on their own."

Unwanted children, children in trouble, can be helped. If you choose to, you can join "Sky King" in coming to their rescue. Look for ways in your own community.

"Whoever receives one such child in My name, receives Me." [MARK 9:37]

Lord, may we befriend youngsters in need.

A SHOP THAT VISITS the shopper has brightened the lives of residents of Wellington Hall Nursing Home in Hackensack, New Jersey.

Many patients had not shopped for gifts or clothing for months or years. Then Joe Wiener of Empire Sales Company brought in his Travelling Store. The home's lounge was transformed with racks of suits, dresses and lingerie. Customers in wheelchairs could shop for slippers, a pantsuit, robe or tie.

"It's a therapy for them," said activities director Lillian Takourian. "Very few of our patients are able to go out. Many haven't been in a department store in years."

The chance to make independent choices also led to a new interest in appearance, said Ms. Takourian.

Visiting shut-ins. Phoning invalids. Writing to prisoners. Small things—until you're on the receiving end. How much of your time—of yourself—could you share with someone? If you make the effort, you won't regret it.

"Comfort one another."
[1 THESSALONIANS 4:18]

℘ Father, show us ways to reach out to the sick, the lonely, the suffering.

SOMETIME IN THE FIRST YEARS of our country, George Washington placed the following want ad in a newspaper:

"Wanted: A Steward for the household of the PRESIDENT of the UNITED STATES. Any person well qualified for and willing to act in this capacity, may learn particulars by inquiring at the President's house, Philadel. Feb. 25."

Did the ad get results? We don't know. But it is significant that the first President of the United States used such ordinary channels to get something done.

It may sound trite to say: "If you want something, ask for it." But it's a sound principle of effective communication.

People can't read minds. We've got to make our legitimate wants and needs known—and turn a sympathetic ear to those of others.

"I will speak noble things, and from my lips will come what is right; for my mouth will utter truth." [PROVERBS 8:6,7]

Holy Spirit, may we be effective instruments of Divine Truth.

ANT SOMEONE TO COLLECT your life insurance early? A "tested and proven recipe" for doing so was suggested by William Williford, director of the New York State Employees Health Maintenance Program:

Take these ingredients daily: 20-40 cigarettes (vary according to taste), six-plus ounces of alcohol, one cup saturated animal fat, one pound carbohydrates, plenty of salt (the more the better), top off with a few diet and/or sleeping pills. Mix well in one average middle-aged adult. Allow to ferment for 10 to 15 years and be sure not to exercise while fermentation is in process.

Body is "done in" when center no longer springs back to the touch.

It's so easy to take health for granted—until we lose it. Care for your body with proper rest, diet and exercise. On these three supports, you can build a life-long and long-life effort to change the world for the better.

> "Health and soundness are better than all gold, and a robust body than countless riches." [SIRACH 30:15]

ε̃ Holy Spirit, may we respect the bodies God has given us.

"**I** DO NOT LIKE NOISE UNLESS I make it myself," runs an old French proverb.

A Connecticut mother admits to what is perhaps an understatement in saying that she and her teenage son have different tastes in music.

They reached a compromise of sorts in sharing the family stereo. But she found it necessary to comment frequently on the loudness of his music and ask that he turn it down. She wondered how young people can stand so much noise. "It must be damaging to their ears," she thought.

She had her comeuppance one day when she was playing her own classical records. Her son came up to her and said, "Mom, it's too loud. Is it okay if I turn it down?"

Startled, she nodded, "Yes." When she realized the difference lay in whose music was being played, she had to chuckle. They laughed together over it.

Laughter can be a good way to communicate. That and the awareness of why we react to each other as we do helps us to live together in harmony.

> "And above all these put on love, which binds everything together in perfect harmony."
>
> [COLOSSIANS 3:14]

Lord, may we have the humility to acknowledge our own foibles.

Some exasperating assumptions about blind people were described by Harold Krents, lawyer and author of the autobiography on which the play "Butterflies Are Free" was based.

Says Mr. Krents: "There are those who assume that since I can't see, I obviously also cannot hear." They either shout at him, he said, or whisper to each other as if he cannot hear at all.

"Others," he adds, "know that of course I can hear, but believe that I can't talk." Waiters ask his wife "what he would like to order."

Still others act as if he needs an interpreter. But, says Mr. Krents, "The toughest misconception of all is the view that because I can't see, I can't work."

Why do we so often assume that blind people can't do certain ordinary tasks? Such assumptions—whatever their cause—are usually groundless.

So let's drop them.

> "Then let us no more pass judgment on one another, but rather decide never to put a stumbling block or hindrance in the way of a brother." [ROMANS 14:13]

℮ Help us accept people as they are, Lord.

ARE YOU A MISER, a spendthrift—or a little of both?
Spending patterns, says behavioral psychologist Dr.
Herbert Fensterheim, are a clue to human personality. He
cites these types of "money madness":

● The miser, who works like a dog, finally makes a
bundle, then doesn't know what to do with it.

● The bargain hunter, who constantly brings home
needless things because they're on sale. He may feel that
the world owes him something for nothing.

● The impulsive spender. He may feel that no one
loves him, so he decides to love himself.

● The happy spendthrift, whose philosophy is "You
might as well spend it while you've got it."

"And," Dr. Fensterheim adds, "you get all kinds of
gradations in between."

Money may—or may not—be the "root of all evil." But
it holds strong power over us. How about you and your
money? A close look may tell you a lot.

"Keep your life free from love of money."
[HEBREWS 13:5]

ᶜᵈ   Jesus, may we seek the treasure that does not
perish—God's favor.

SHIRLEY AND WALT SHAW run one of the most popular bars in La Habra, California—and it's non-alcoholic.

Called Hawby's Habit, the cheerful tavern has the
elements of a successful bar, but caters to people who
prefer not to go to regular bars.

The Shaws, both recovered alcoholics, missed the gai-
ety and music of tavern surroundings. So they opened
their unique bar, where they serve Margaritas, Bloody
Marys and other drinks—all non-alcoholic. There are
barstools, booths and even a tiny dance floor.

"I'd say that half our crowds are recovered alcoholics,"
says Mrs. Shaw. "But we get a lot of people who just don't
drink. Church groups. Young people."

In our society, it's not easy to be someone who "just
doesn't drink." If we respect the divine gift of freedom,
we'll be careful not to force our views and ways of doing
things on others. One way is to be sure to have plenty of
non-alcoholic beverages on hand when we give a party.

"Live, and walk in the way of insight."
[PROVERBS 9:6]

Grant us the sensitivity, Jesus, to know when
not to "push."

Much will be written about Hubert Humphrey, the durable senator from Minnesota and former vice president. Here's one incident, a small one. Or is it?

After the diagnosis of an inoperable tumor and a period of hospitalization, a considerably thinner Senator Humphrey made his first appearance in public.

The 66-year-old senator was speaking to the Minnesota AFL-CIO convention.

"I'm not about ready," he said, "to have somebody cover me up." There wasn't a dry eye in the hall. And the senator was no exception.

"Muriel warned me that they'd be taking my picture if I wiped my eyes," he commented, referring to his wife. "But so what? Let them take it. A man with no tears is a man with no heart."

Perhaps there are times when a "stiff upper lip" is an appropriate response to pain and sorrow. But too often, we suppress our tears in the face of life's bruises. Remember: "A man with no tears is a man with no heart."

> "My compassion grows warm and tender."
> [HOSEA 11:8]

   ᏋᏋ   Jesus, You were a man in touch with human feelings. Show us the way.

The ELDERLY WATCH more television than any other adult age group in America. Mount Sinai School of Medicine in New York is using this fact to spread health information to the inner city's older population..

With foundation funding, all elderly tenants of Gaylord White Public Housing in East Harlem received free cable outlets for a special channel. Nine weekly programs are cablecast.

Daily features include health care information, a slot where tenants read inspirational messages or poems, and a "Know Your Neighbor" segment introducing project residents.

Viewers are enthusiastic.

The potential of television to meet the real needs of people has hardly been tried. And, on commercial TV, it probably never will. Other outlets, such as cable, may have a greater chance to succeed. But that requires public insistence on the public being served.

"...but having in view the welfare, both public and private, of all the people."

[2 MACCABEES 4:5]

Spur us to have every form of communication, Holy Spirit, to meet and help people where they are.

ARCHITECTURE STUDENTS at Rensselaer Polytechnic Institute in Troy, New York, are building a "garbage house."

Using tin cans, cardboard newsprint tubes, soda bottles and metal package strapping, the class is building a four-room cottage which Professor Dora Crouch has bought and plans to live in. Its cost—$600.

The house, with walls of tin cans mortared like bricks and a "window wall" of vari-colored bottles, was designed by London Professor Martin Pauley. It will be insulated with a foot-thick layer of textile mill waste threads. The structure will be as strong and fireproof as a conventional wood-frame house.

"I was very concerned about the incredible cost of housing," says Professor Pauley, "and thought there may be ways of reducing it drastically through the use of waste products."

The creativity of the designer of such a house is considerable. It is inspired by human need. Can you encourage ingenuity in providing housing for the poor in your community?

"Let us rise up and build." [NEHEMIAH 2:18]

  Help me, Father, to see where there is need and to meet the challenge it presents.

IMAGINE TELLING A COMPUTER your vacation plans: "I'm going by car. I want to fish and photograph old churches." Zip! Click! Out comes a customized map showing the best route to take.

Or picture a fire fighter alerted to a brush fire. He dashes to a computer and enters location, wind speed, temperature and other pertinent data. In seconds, out chatters a projection of where the fire will be in six hours, giving time to plot strategies for fighting the blaze.

Dreams? Not at all, says Hollis Vail, a mapmaker with the Department of the Interior. These maps and others equally revolutionary already exist in some cases. Soon they will be in common use.

We're unquestionably getting better at mapping our physical world, thanks to advanced computers and monitoring by satellites. But what about choosing the path for our spiritual journey? God has repeatedly communicated "the way, the truth and the life." Do we look at His map?

> "I will instruct you and teach you the way you should go. I will counsel you with my eye upon you." [PSALM 32:8]

ℰ   Lord, guide us on our journey to You.

ORATIO ALGER HAS NOTHING on newspaper boy Paul Shubert. Paul's fortune grew from $4 to $9 million with one click of a computer.

The 14-year-old carrier for the *Philadelphia Bulletin* deposited his $4 earnings in his bank account. That night when he opened his bank book he saw that the bank's computer had credited him with $9,999,004.

"I just kept looking at it for a minute," said Paul. "I couldn't believe it."

Returning to the bank after showing the book to his mother, Paul pointed out the error. He didn't ask for a reward.

"What would they give me a reward for?" he commented. "I just want to keep this bank book."

However brief, what a thrill Paul Shubert must have gotten out of being declared a millionaire. You and I may never get that pleasure—real or imaginary. But every day we get a gift money can't buy—another new day of life. Cherish it. Use it.

> "Rejoice in all the good which the Lord your God has given to you and to your house."
> [DEUTERONOMY 26:11]

Holy Spirit, fill us with a joy for living.

IT TOOK TEENAGERS to solve the problem of graffiti on the walls of a housing project.

After the high, wide walls of Los Angeles' Estrada Courts project were repeatedly defaced, teenagers who lived there suggested painting murals on the walls. The Housing Authority supplied approval and the paint. The Fire Department gave scaffolding. Three murals grew to 18, 22, and 51, finished and sealed in protective coating.

By 1973, 151 youngsters and supervisors were receiving full or partial salaries for this work through summer programs and Employment and Training Act grants. The murals, used in the opening and closing footage of NBC's "Chico and the Man," paid off in community pride and youth activities.

It's easier to talk about guiding youthful energies than to do it. But there's a lot to be said for helping direct young people's powers. Suppression just doesn't work. Encouragement sometimes does. So which is worth the effort?

"Exhort one another every day."
[HEBREWS 3:13]

Remind us when we need it most, Holy Spirit, to think and act in a positive manner.

ANET KANCYLAR IS ALWAYS up to her elbows in her work. She has to be. She's a dishwasher.

As one of the most specialized and highly paid dishwashers in the country, Mrs. Kancylar scrubs the flasks used in scientific experiments at the Laurence Livermore Laboratory in Livermore, California.

"And believe me, the scientists are very fussy about their glassware," says Mrs. Kancylar. Hundreds of pieces are gathered every morning and thoroughly scoured by the dishwashers. After rinsing, they are loaded into an automatic dishwasher and rinsed three more times. Then the beakers and test tubes are dried, packed in plastic, and returned to the labs.

Mrs. Kancylar explains the painstaking procedure, "If any slight trace of mold or even detergent is left on a flask, it can ruin an entire experiment."

It's so easy to overlook small details, to do less than our best. A lack of attention to detail can alter an experiment, a relationship, a job, a life. Little things can make a big difference.

"He who despises small things will fail little by little." [SIRACH 19:1]

Father, let us take time for little things.

A 13-YEAR-OLD BOY in Kenosha, Wisconsin, found that big-city officialdom has a heart.

Ronnie Thomas is a beer can collector. To add to his treasure of 1,148 different containers—some 40 years old—he ordered a six-pack of Alpine Ryingerbrau from England. Then things got complicated.

Federal laws prohibit the mailing of alcoholic beverages, so United States Customs claimed the package. Then a notice went out to Ronnie: A duty of 29 cents was due and the cans had to be picked up in New York.

So his mother turned to City Hall for help. Soon they got word that the Mayor's action center had picked up the cans, emptied their contents and was sending them to Ronnie.

"New York must be a wonderful place," wrote Mrs. Thomas, "to have people such as you with such big hearts."

Despite glum assessments of our world, there is much caring to be found. Someone cared about Ronnie Thomas. We can all give joy by caring more.

"Make love your aim." [1 CORINTHIANS 14:1]

e₂ You showed us by Your example, Jesus, how to love one another. May we remember.

WHILE HELPING WITH "Operation Babylift," Nebraska State Senator John DeCamp adopted two Vietnamese boys and set in motion the reuniting of a family.

Back in Nebraska, the senator learned of a Vietnamese refugee who fit the description of the boys' mother. After a long search he located her with her other two children in South Carolina.

He learned that, in the last Communist push, her American husband had been ordered home and couldn't get his family out. Later, the woman, escaping with her four children and other refugees, was separated from her sons. She reached this country thinking she would never see them again.

Now, the whole family is together in South Carolina—largely through John DeCamp's efforts.

Jesus spoke to His disciples about the concern of the Father for them—even more than for the birds of the air and the lilies of the field. He surely had in mind, also, our concern for each other—our part in doing His work.

"Always seek to do good to one another."
[1 THESSALONIANS 5:16]

ↄ̃ 　 May we obey Your command, Lord, to love one another. Only then will Your Will be done.

BRUCE JENNINGS PEDALLED a 15-speed bike for six weeks to cross a continent—with one leg.

After losing a leg in a motorcycle smashup, Mr. Jennings, 24, felt that he had to "do something to prove to myself that I wasn't finished. I decided to ride across the country."

The young Californian sustained two more accidents while learning to ride his bicycle. Run over by a car, he nearly lost his other leg and suffered a punctured lung and ruptured spleen. Then he started training again.

Finally he began—at Newport Beach, California. He averaged over 100 miles a day, reaching New York in 39 days. He did what he set out to do. Now he plans to get on with his life.

We all admire such determination. We each, with God's help, have to "run our own race." The challenge is not to compare ourselves with others. But to live up to the best that is in us.

> "Let us run with perseverance the race that is set before us." [HEBREWS 12:1]

Let us be helped by what others accomplish, Jesus.

THE WISH TO BE WORKING—with or without pay—was high on the list of priorities in a recent Louis Harris survey of people over 65.

Pollster Harris told reporters that a study for the National Council on the Aging showed that the nation's aged feel they are being misused. Almost one-fourth of the 4,254 persons polled said they wanted jobs.

Concluded Mr. Harris: "It is time for the establishment in America to wake up and realize there is a vast untapped potential of solid energy out there which does not want to be dumped on the scrap heap of inactivity." He also warned, "We shall see a wave of militance among senior citizens as their numbers rise."

There is never a good excuse for letting people's talents go unused. Can you make a start in your community to harness the tremendous potential of retirees? Give it some thought—and some prayer.

"Rich experience is the crown of the aged."
[SIRACH 25:6]

ℰℰ May we be creative, Lord, in helping all to contribute.

A GEORGIA PSYCHOLOGIST DECIDED to improve his seminars for parents by taking a step backward.

Dr. Roy Kern believes that, before sessions on child rearing can be effective, the parents need to know themselves. His program, "Maintaining Sanity in Your Life and Home," starts there.

The psychologist then moves on to family dynamics—how family life influences children—and, finally, to the "nuts and bolts" of child rearing. The program also points out to parents their potential for change.

Referring to the increase in mental illness, divorce and alcoholism, Dr. Kern notes, "We spend millions of dollars on cures for our problems but very little money goes for prevention."

We influence children—or anyone—by what we are rather than by techniques. Most of us, however, travel a rocky road toward the goal of becoming effective, well-adjusted people. Techniques help. But, remember, love is the main ingredient.

"So faith, hope, love abide, these three; but the greatest of these is love."
[1 CORINTHIANS 13:13]

ᏋᏋ Fill us with Your Spirit, Lord, so we will be the loving human beings we were made to be.

OPPORTUNITIES, says a *Royal Bank of Canada Letter,* don't arrive labelled with your name and instructions for using them. But they do arrive, for everyone. Here are the Letter's tips for using them:

● Don't wait for the "big opportunity." Small opportunities may expand.

● Keep in touch with what is going on, and be open-minded to new notions and ideas.

● Locate a real need. Check out the difficulties. Collect information. List the benefits. Then produce the answer.

● Translate your plan into action as soon as possible.

● Do something beyond your regular and assigned duties. Opportunities are found through the "little extras."

● Difficulties beset all beginnings. Persist.

Start each day with a passive, ho-hum attitude and nothing much will probably happen. Get up with a desire to mine your waking hours for the ore of opportunity, and you'll be surprised by the number of challenges you find.

> "As we have opportunity, let us do good to all men." [GALATIANS 6:10]

℮ Jesus, You constantly sought challenges to do the Father's will. May we do the same.

A "BUG" WITH A HEALTHY APPETITE for oil may offer hope for cleaning up oil spills.

The oil-eating microbe with the jaw-breaking name "multi-plasmid hydrocarbon-degrading pseudomonas" was developed by microbiologist Ananda Chakrabarty, after six years of research. Combining four strains of bacteria, Dr. Chakrabarty produced a "superbug" that can consume and break down the hydrocarbons in oil.

In laboratory tests, a pinch of the organisms will eat an eye dropper-full of oil in a few days. They offer evidence that they may be developed into an effective way of dealing with oil pollution.

Such a bug is one way to cope with oil spills. Another would be to press legislators to exercise great caution before granting the right to drill in offshore waters.

Earth's resources are limited. Our ingenuity is not—or scarcely so. To protect God's creation for those who come after us is a gift to the future.

> "For the Lord has made all things, and to the godly He has granted wisdom."
>
> [SIRACH 43:33]

ﻉ   Make us more conservation-minded, Father, so that all may enjoy Your bounty.

A RIDE IN A NEW YORK TAXI may move some of the city's 400,000 alcoholics to seek help.

The taxicab industry is enlisting its cabbies in a drive to alert problem drinkers. Stickers placed in thousands of cabs announce: "Alcoholism is a treatable disease. For help or information call (212) 935-7070."

"Drivers are frightened of alcoholics," explains Robert Scull, owner of a 135-cab fleet. "A driver who has an alcoholic in the back of his cab is in danger."

The emergency phone number reaches the National Council on Alcoholism. There, trained workers refer callers to treatment centers.

The first step in solving a problem is to recognize that help is needed. The second is to seek it and accept it.

Whether any of us decides to ask for assistance is up to us. But we can be God's instruments for good by providing realistic, hopeful information to those who can use it.

> "You yourselves are full of goodness, filled with all knowledge, and able to instruct one another." [ROMANS 15:14]

 e̓ Make us agents of enlightenment, Lord, in every encounter of our lives.

A 12-YEAR-OLD BOY WAS SAVED from suffocation in a sand hopper when a gravel pit worker clung to him for 50 minutes until firemen came.

The Salt Lake City, Utah, youngster fell into the working hopper after being warned to stay clear of the machinery. By the time pit-hand Andy Cruz dived in and grabbed him, all but his head had disappeared into the rushing sand. While a co-worker rushed to turn off the hopper, Mr. Cruz's wife called police and firemen.

The boy was freed and taken to a nearby hospital where he was treated for shock.

"He was getting pretty heavy and I was getting pretty tired by the time they pulled him free," the rescuer said afterward.

Some people see a need and rush right into action to do as much as they can. Others fuss and fret while valuable moments tick by.

Are you a "doer" or a "stewer"? It can make a big difference.

> "Be doers of the word, and not hearers only."
> [JAMES 1:22]

e² Father, make us prompt to respond in time of crisis.

THE OCCUPATION OF PROFESSIONAL page-turner is probably not among those dreamed about.

It's not what Louis Yelnick of Brooklyn dreamed about either. He had youthful visions of himself at the piano, captivating concert audiences. But he never made it. He admits he "wasn't any good."

Instead, Mr. Yelnick spends his days as a shoe specialist in Macy's sporting goods department. At night he turns pages for professional musicians.

The job has problems: missing cues and stuck pages. And Mr. Yelnick has to soothe artists who are bothered by the noise of turning pages.

But for little more than two hours' work, he earns $25 and he says, "I get to hear a lot of beautiful music that I would ordinarily have to pay for."

Dreams can make things happen. But they have to face the test of reality. And sometimes they have to be changed. Seek out your talents. Build on them. Remember, there's nobody like you.

> "For everything here is a season and a time for every matter under heaven."
>
> [ECCLESIASTES 3:1]

Help me, Father, to understand that my failure may be an opportunity in disguise.

Two young women, a Catholic and a Protestant, launched three peace marches in strife-torn Belfast that brought 30,000 to 40,000 people together.

Mrs. Betty Williams and Miss Mairead Corrigan organized the walks after the killing of three children added to the over 1,600 lives lost by the warring of Protestant and Catholic factions in northern Ireland.

Arm-in-arm, hundreds of families of the two faiths walked together to Belfast's Woodvale Park, where Mrs. Williams led the crowd in the "Declaration of the Peace People." Many in the group wept openly.

A reporter, while noting that the fighting has not yet ended, called the marches a "vast outpouring of popular feeling and revulsion against the violence... a miracle in Belfast."

To seek peace is not for the weak or the timid. The road to enduring peace is through the practice of justice. It requires dedication, perseverance and love. No wonder the peacemakers are called "blessed."

> "And He came and preached peace to you who were far off and peace to those who were near." [EPHESIANS 2:17]

℮ Despite wars, misunderstandings and family disputes, Lord, move us to be peacemakers in thought and action.

BECAUSE OF NEW TECHNIQUES, the 10,000 babies born each year in the United States with heart defects now have a chance to live.

In a process called hypotherma, pioneered in Canada, New Zealand and Japan, newly born infants are packed in ice to lower body temperature to 20 degrees C for open heart surgery. Widely used for the past few years, the technique gives surgeons a non-beating heart to operate on without risk of brain damage.

"This is a new chapter in heart surgery," says Dr. Charles Hatcher, professor of surgery at Emory University. Previously, he said, "a child born with a heart defect had to wait until he weighed 25 or 30 pounds before we could operate." Now, said the doctor, surgical units can operate on 24-hour standby for immediate correction of heart defects in newborns.

Science fulfills its divinely intended purpose when technical competence serves the cause of life.

Do you follow news of scientific accomplishments? Or pray that scientists use their talents responsibly?

"As each has received a gift, employ it for one another." [1 PETER 4:10]

Spur us to employ our own gifts and abilities, Holy Spirit, in a manner that will assist others.

THE NEWSGATHERING SKILLS used by reporters can help anyone to listen more effectively:

- *Understand.* Listen as though you must report on what is being said. Listen for the whys, whens, hows.
- *What's the point?* Can you reduce what is being said to a single, clear statement?
- *Consider motives.* What is the person really saying? Is he communicating or has he an ax to grind?
- *Concentrate fully on the speaker.*
- *Clarify.* Don't be afraid to ask questions about confusing statements.
- *Take notes.* In appropriate situations, note names, places, dates, spelling, phrases.
- *Learn to "turn off" gracefully.* Be tactful, creative— and firm. Show appreciation.

Do you find that you quickly forget what others say to you? Maybe your listening skills are a little rusty. Why not brighten them today?

"An attentive ear is the wise man's desire."
[SIRACH 3:29]

Help us to learn, Father, that we have to understand before we can care.

A YOUNGSTER HELPING her little brother at school inspired a unique educational experiment at San Diego's Peace Elementary School.

The program groups students with "teachers" who are their older brothers, sisters or cousins. Children from kindergarten to sixth grade work together, with older children teaching their younger siblings.

"We really try to follow the philosophy that everyone is a teacher," says program developer Joyce Chapman. "The kindergarteners are doing well because they never have to feel they are lost at school. The older ones have developed very positive self-images and feelings of responsibility." Commented one pleased mother:

"My kids have tried to keep up with each other in sports. Now my youngest brings home oodles of homework so he can be like his older brother and sister."

Children helping other children may be one of the most overlooked educational tools we have. Encourage your youngsters to be "givers" as well as "receivers." It will enable them to grow—and others, too.

"It is more blessed to give than to receive."
[ACTS 20:35]

ᏩᏁ Grant us a greater realization, Father, of the ways in which we can assist others to do—and be—better.

IN THE SPRING OF 1978, in California, the desert bloomed. It hadn't happened for six years.

After a winter in which the entire normal year's rainfall fell in six weeks, suddenly a carpet of flowers covered the desert with brilliant color.

The seeds of desert flowers have the capacity to remain dormant for years at a time under merciless summer sun and dry desert winters. Then, in optimum conditions, they spring into life once again, blooming profusely as though they could hardly wait.

The phenomenon is symbolic of what can happen after the dry desert times in human experience—if we don't give up hope:

Hope in God, who doesn't seem to answer our prayers.

Hope in those close to us who seem not to be listening, or have taken an alien path, or who themselves are close to despair.

Hope in ourselves, in our own capacity for rebirth.

Is there someone you can help to hope again?

> "Hope does not disappoint us, because God's love has been poured in our hearts."
>
> [ROMANS 5:5]

Lord, where there is despair let me bring hope.

A MAN WHO TOOK GREAT PRIDE in his lawn found himself with a large crop of dandelions.

He tried every method he knew to get rid of them. Still they plagued him.

Finally, he wrote to the Department of Agriculture. He enumerated all the things he had tried and closed his letter with the question, "What shall I do now?"

In due course came the reply, "We suggest you learn to love them."

We all face things that exasperate us. And often, despite our best efforts, they "won't go away."

It may take a major turnabout to accept what we can't change but that switch can bring some surprises: relief, peace, perspective, even an unexpected solution.

How about people who plague us? Learning to love them may be a little harder than accepting dandelions, but the effort can bring the deep joy and peace Jesus promised us if we follow His way.

> "And this is love, that we follow His commandments... that we follow love."
>
> [1 JOHN 1:6]

ᐱ Lord, teach me the power of love.

WALKING IS SOMETHING SPECIAL for John Kormylo, ever since an accident he had as a child.

"I was helping another kid steal coal," he said. "His family needed it." It was during the Depression. A freight car ran over John's foot.

A surgeon amputated his leg below the knee and fitted him with an artificial limb.

Now as a prosthetist himself, Mr. Kormylo makes artificial limbs for amputees. He's "been there" and wants to help. So far, he has made over 75,000 prosthetic devices.

"One of the most rewarding things is to see amputees happiness when they walk almost normally for the first time," he says. "Their faces change, their outlook changes, their life is better."

John Kormylo could have gone through life bitter about the loss of a limb. Instead, he turned it into a motive for serving others. He lighted a candle rather than curse the darkness.

> "Satisfy the desire of the afflicted, then shall your light rise in the darkness."
>
> [ISAIAH 58:10

꒦ Holy Spirit, show us how to turn life's adversities into triumphs.

BECAUSE OF THE GENTLE ATTENTION of a group of ex-drug offenders, hundreds of shut-in elderly New Yorkers are enjoying trips and excursions.

In a program called Easy Ride, the ex-offenders receive training in driving defensively and assisting the handicapped. Selected through the Wildcat Corp., a non-profit organization of ex-offenders, candidates must demonstrate a special sensitivity in working with the handicapped. Once trained, they escort aged and disabled citizens on weekly trips—to visit families, perform errands, or attend entertainments.

"For me it's a lovely idea," said one wheelchair-bound woman who can now visit her sister each week. For her, and for other residents, Easy Ride has brought freedom from the fear of being mugged and from the boredom of long days spent alone in their apartments.

Former drug offenders can be good citizens. Somebody, obviously, has to believe in them before the trust can pay off. Is there someone in your life that a little well-placed trust could give a lift?

> "Hold fast to what is good; love one another with brotherly affection." [ROMANS 12:9]

eĉ Aid us to trust others, Jesus, without being gullible.

HARD WORK MAY BE ONE WAY to success, but psychologist David A. Travland, 34, says too much work can be harmful if it isn't balanced by a reasonably good home life.

How can you tell if you're on the job too much and at home too little? Internally, your stomach will tell you; you'll feel frustrated, discontent. Externally, your boss and family will let you know if you're off target, says Dr. Travland.

After spotting the problem, then what? Don't work even harder at a solution. Set goals and a strategy to reach them. See how you've been using and misusing your time, he recommends.

Too much work can be as bad as too little. It can be a way of ducking other—more personal—responsibilities. Far from being heroic, it may actually be the easy way out.

Even work suffers—to say nothing of closeness to oneself, one's family and one's God—when we make it an idol.

> "Do not labor for the food which perishes, but for the food which endures to eternal life."
> [JOHN 6:27]

 Guide us, Holy Spirit, into the way of moderation that strikes a balance in all areas of our lives.

THERE'S A NATIONAL ORGANIZATION which exists to offer help and support to this country's estimated 100,000 dwarfs and midgets.

Often these persons have problems with such things as elevator buttons, pay telephones, even having a satisfying social life. Situations which are routine for most can become obstacles for little people. And the Little Peoples Association is there to help, says a former president, 4-foot-6 Charles Bedow.

"We've got to get to the architects first and we've got to get to the 5-year-olds to train them how to think and operate in a big world," Mr. Bedow said. He expects it will take decades before little people are fully accommodated in everyday life. But LPA keeps growing.

LPA is hard at work promoting very constructive solutions to a very real need. How about you? Do you "curse the darkness"? Or do you look for ways to light at least one small candle?

> "If we walk in the light . . . we have fellowship with one another."　　　　[1 JOHN 1:7]

ℰℰ　Holy Spirit, guide us into constructive courses of action.

FOR ASPIRING DO-IT-YOURSELFERS, one company makes sure that help is just a phone call away.

With a unique hot-line for puzzled customers, Heathkit Electronic Centers' Fair Lawn, New Jersey, store has five electricians taking calls for two hours daily. Guiding customers through mazes of instructions for hundreds of kits, the technicians answer questions about misconnected discs and transistors, shorted circuits, and a host of other electronic problems.

The company issues instruction manuals up to five volumes long for catalogue items, ranging from an $8.95 lightbulb dimmer to a $699.95 color television. But, says service manager Ernie Wolitzer, that isn't always enough: "The idea is to sell kits and help people put them together."

Wouldn't it be great if we had a hot-line to use every time our lives became unmanageable? In a sense, we do. It's called prayer. Use it. God never turns a deaf ear to those who seek Him in faith.

> "Lift up your face to God...make your prayer to Him, and He will hear you."
>
> [JOB 22:26,27]

✐ Jesus, help us to stay close to the Father.

EVERY DAY JOHN FILOPOWICZ sees brightly colored beetles, giant spiders, big bats, butterflies and owls in the middle of Chicago. He sees them from his perch as operator of the window washing machine atop the 110-story Sears Tower.

Mr. Filopowicz rides on hoists that move on tracks to lower and raise the automatic washer sprays that wash the building's hundreds of windows.

"I see something new up here every day," he says. "Colonies of yellow-striped beetles cling to TV antennas at the very top. Spiders with a body the size of a quarter have webs, and large bats hang there. Moths with wingspreads of seven inches visit the roof-tops. At times beautiful butterflies hover around. The other day, a white-gray owl floated up on the updraft, looked at me and flew around to the other side."

What we see is largely determined by where we sit. We may not care to be 110 stories high, but we can try to get our world—our life—into perspective. Prayer to God is one way to get a bigger picture.

"Look at what is before your eyes."
[2 CORINTHIANS 10:7]

Widen our horizons, Holy Spirit, as we live from day to day.

At NEW YORK'S PLAZA HOTEL, ringing for the bell man is a thing of the past. When Kathleen Shearer joined the staff of bellhops at the aristocratic old hotel, the Plaza officially switched the title to "bellperson."

Ms. Shearer, 25, had been a waitress at the Plaza' Palm Court restaurant, "the nicest waitressing job I ever had," she said, "but I wanted to see what the rooms at the Plaza looked like."

How did she convince the Plaza to try her as a bellperson? According to her supervisor, Tom Mylonas, it was her firm handshake, which was "a good indication of hand and arm strength" for carrying luggage.

A firm handshake might indicate not only a "carrying person" but a "caring person." And the world needs caring persons who are mindful of the needs of the poor, the suffering, the distressed. Haven't you needed a caring person? That's as it should be—and you can always be one too.

> "Let your compassion come speedily to meet us." [PSALM 79:8]

Lord, help me to remember how it is to be in need, and to be mindful of those who are in need.

"**G**OSSIP" IS DEFINED in the dictionary as an "idle tattler;" "newsmonger;" and also as one who spreads "groundless rumor."

An unknown author had this to say on the subject: "My name is Gossip. I have no respect for justice; I ruin without killing; I tear down homes; I break hearts and wreck lives. I am wily, cunning, malicious, and I gather strength with age. I make my way where greed, mistrust, and dishonor are unknown. I feed on good and bad alike. My victims are as numerous as the sands of the sea, and often as innocent. I never forgive and seldom forget. My name is Gossip."

Man was created by God to live and work with his fellow man, not to hurt him; to build up, not tear down; to draw people together in love, not to separate them by strife.

If we catch in flight the impulses to be unkind and change it to a charitable word or action, we would make a big difference in the world. Isn't it worth the effort?

> "Keep your tongue from evil, and your lips from speaking deceit." [PSALMS 34:13]

Lord, teach me to help, not hurt those around me.

Deanna Edwards of Bloomington, Illinois, provides comfort for the old and the ill. Her voice and her guitar are all she needs.

As a music therapist, she went into the hospital room of one elderly man to sing a song for him. "Your song was fine," he told her, "but I'd rather talk."

So she listened and she later wrote this song:

"It's been a long, long time since I've said what's on my mind.

"Doesn't anybody have the time to spare?

"I have memories I wish that I could share.

"Is there someone who will listen to an old man

"Though they've heard the words a hundred times before?

"All the stories I have told, like me, are growing old . . .

"Doesn't anybody listen anymore?"

In time of trouble, the most precious gift you can give a friend may be your ability just to listen. At any time, real listening nourishes you *and* the other person.

> "If you will not listen; my soul will weep in secret." [JEREMIAH 13:17]

ᘒ Help me, Lord, to listen with an open heart.

THE CHILDREN OF SAN MATEO County, California, know magic when they see it.

Jerry Sowers, 16, of Ron's Hocus-Pocus Magic Shop demonstrates rope, coin and card tricks for the youngsters who often crowd into the store. The magician makes things jump, disappear, shorten, lengthen, and multiply to the wonder of his audience.

"A lot of the time," Jerry says, "the kids come in and say, 'I don't have any money but show me a magic trick.' So I entertain them. It's good practice for me."

Ron Ehrmantraut, owner of Hocus-Pocus and also an amateur magician, hired the boy. He thought it would be fun to have a teenager work with the children.

"Everybody likes magic," Jerry agrees. "It's nice to believe in something you know can't be real."

"Believing" magic tricks is fun. But real faith—in God, ourselves and each other—can add strength, meaning and peace to our lives.

That's *really* something!

"Have faith in God."　　　　[MARK 11:22]

ɛᵌ　Father, deepen my faith in You.

A NEED FOR VEGETABLES in their scant welfare diet led to a booming business for Lloyd and Cory Merriman seven years ago.

The Colorado couple went on public assistance when illness forced Mr. Merriman off his job. They began a backyard garden to supplement their meagre income. Their first tomato crop yielded a surplus which they sold. With the profits, they built one, two, then finally five greenhouse additions on their one-acre plot.

Now selling 20,000 boxes of flowers, plants and vegetables to nearly 20 western Colorado communities, the Merrimans claim "the biggest assortment of house plants in Colorado." Says Mrs. Merriman proudly, "Any seed I can get hold of, I grow it."

Most people want to be self-supporting and productive. They aren't looking for handouts. Sometimes it takes imagination, effort—and maybe an outside assist—to produce economic independence. Is there someone you can help—today?

> "Let our people learn to apply themselves to good deeds, so as to help in cases of urgent need." [TITUS 3:14]

❧ Father, may we be concerned for each other's welfare.

IF YOU THINK YOUR CHILD would benefit from summer camp, and you've decided on the type of camp, then health and camping officials suggest asking:

What experience do the director and employees have? How many children will one counselor supervise? Are the camp and its vehicles free of hazards? Is the camp sanitary? What are the cabins like? What about food preparation areas? Nutrition? Do campers and staff have to present health histories and evidence of recent checkups and innoculations? Is there a nurse present? A doctor on call? Were any severe injuries or deaths reported to the Health Department? How often can you call or visit?

Summer camp—carefully chosen and properly supervised—can be a rewarding experience for a youngster. An important step in the process is a parent—or parents—who does the proper homework.

If you're picking a camp, do so responsibly.

> "Let everyone be fully convinced in his own mind." [ROMANS 14:5]

e❧ Lord, guide those parents who are selecting a camp for their children.

IF YOUR CAR BREAKS DOWN in Pound Ridge, New York, you're in luck. A couple of car-doctors there make house calls—and bring repair service with them.

Judy Bevans and Bruce Buccarelli are the owner-operators of "Shade Tree Fix-It," a mobile auto repair shop. Their van contains $15,000 worth of sophisticated equipment so they can do any car repairs without moving the car.

When Mrs. Bevans met Mr. Buccarelli, an experienced mechanic, she expressed dissatisfaction with the auto repair business. He promised to show her how to care for her own car. The idea of the mobile van came about gradually.

Judy Bevans believes "the real value of our service is that we can fix your car right on the spot."

There are times when we can serve another person as no one else can. Times when our family, friends, even strangers need us. Do we take that extra step to be "right on the spot?"

"Through love be servants of one another."
[GALATIANS 5:13]

⟨ꭰ⟩ Make us more aware of opportunities to serve, Lord.

Georgian Martha Harper, a great-grandmother in her sixties, turned carpenter after her husband died.

"To keep from worrying and grieving," Mrs. Harper, with no prior knowledge of carpentry, donned her husband's coveralls and finished a picket fence he had started before he died.

Since then she has added to her home a wooden patio, kitchen cabinets and a basement bedroom. She follows a picture or, in the case of the cabinets, just looks at the existing ones.

"I don't know how I can do it anymore than you do," says Mrs. Harper about her work. "I guess I just like to be creative."

She also sews, but doing that sometimes makes her "jittery." "When I get this way," she says, "I start working on the carpentry. Then I see myself progress . . . and I feel like a million dollars."

One way to keep from "worrying and grieving" may be to find your own unfinished picket fence and get to work.

"Cast all your anxieties on Him, for He cares about you." [1 PETER 5:7]

 Help us, Father, to find alternatives to self-pity.

ARTISTS WHO ARE DOWN on their luck may now be in luck if they need medical assistance.

Change, Inc., led by painter Robert Rauschenberg, has formalized a barter system with several hospitals in New York, Texas and California. The group collects prints and paintings donated by artists and collectors. Participating hospitals select those they want to brighten their walls. The equivalent dollar value of the works is provided in medical services.

At Manhattan's Hospital for Joint Diseases the first $250,000 worth of art will cover medical care for up to 70 artists. More donations are expected.

As for the applicants for assistance, Mr. Rauschenberg insists, "We never judge an artist on aesthetic grounds." They need only show that they're sick, broke and in the arts.

Barter is one way of using an old idea to solve a current problem. But it takes imagination, organization and co-operation to make it work. Ideas, no matter how good, need planning to turn them into practical solutions.

> "He who had received the five talents went at once and traded with them; and he made five talents more." [MATTHEW 25:16]

Teach me, Holy Spirit, to use my ability in the service of others.

How OFTEN DO WE LABEL a person by a single experience?

To make a judgment based on what may be an atypical episode can lead to distorted perception. *Executives' Digest* gives some ideas that can clarify them:

1. Knowing yourself makes it easier to see others accurately.

2. Your own characteristics are likely to influence what you see in others.

3. If you're comfortable with yourself, you're more likely to appreciate others.

4. If you like somebody, odds are that you'll be inclined to notice the ways in which he or she resembles you. Conversely, you'll try to widen the gap between you and someone you don't like by exaggerating the points of dissimilarity.

People are too complex to be defined by a single incident—a good thing to remember the next time we're tempted to make hasty judgments.

"Hasty judgment has led many astray."

[SIRACH 3:24]

ce   Father, may we learn not to judge one another.

FIFTY HUNGRY PEOPLE gathered on a Palm Sunday evening in an upstate New York church to pray—and munch apples, cheese and crackers after a 24-hour fast.

From teenagers to retired older people, they were members of Bread for the World. In tune with the aims of that organization which lobbies for the hungry, they fasted as a way to examine their Christian responsibility in a culture of over-consumption.

For some this was not new. Every week, Janice Fitzgerald, a young homemaker, fasts from supper of one day until breakfast a day and a half later. She figures how much money she saves and gives that amount to causes that fight hunger.

"I can just say from my own experience," says Mrs. Fitzgerald, of prayerful fasting, "that it makes you feel clean in body and spirit."

To experience temporarily the pangs and energy loss of hunger is to glimpse how it is with millions of people most of the time. Understanding can lead to compassion. But you have to take the first step.

> "All her people groan as they search for bread, they trade their treasures for food to revive their strength." [LAMENTATIONS 1:11]

> Help me, Jesus, to do something about the plight of my brothers and sisters who are hungry.

HUMANE SOCIETY OFFICIALS in Minneapolis are convinced that the fun of having a bunny sitting in your home Easter morning is easier on the bunnies if families rent the rabbits instead of buying them. So the society rents them.

"The novelty (of owning a rabbit) is very fleeting," says veterinarian Dr. William Mahr. "Kids tend to ignore them after a week. Doors are slammed on them."

Dr. George Mather, professor of veterinary medicine, agrees that the thrill of having a live rabbit quickly wears off.

"Easter morning is great," he says, "but the day after it's the mother's duty."

Something that at first seems like a good idea may, in fact, have a very short life span. It pays to check alternatives. And if you can't find any, consider developing some of your own. You have to strike a match to light a candle.

> "You are my lamp, O Lord, and my God lightens my darkness." [2 SAMUEL 22:29]

Father, open our eyes wide to the possibilities for constructive action.

WORRIES WEIGH DOWN many persons because they refuse to face them, suggests theologian, Dr. Oswald Hoffman. He proposes the following:

1. Regard troubles as real, don't dismiss anxieties as "all in the mind."

2. Don't blame your problems on others.

3. Remember you're not alone, we've all got troubles.

4. Regard some problems as opportunities.

5. Seek expert advice if you can't go it alone.

6. Re-think, maybe even change, your goals.

7. Reserve time for yourself regularly. A little contemplation can focus your activities.

Remember what an unknown sage said about the waste of worrying, "ninety-nine percent of the things people worry about never happen. The other one percent are unavoidable."

Worry will never get us anywhere. And it robs us of the energy to do what we have to do now. Take care of today—it's all we have.

> "Therefore do not be anxious about tomorrow, for tomorrow will be anxious for itself."
> [MATTHEW 6:34

ε๊   Give us, Lord, a deeper trust in You.

A COUNSELOR at the University of Tampa, Florida, 26-year-old Tom Balistrieri gets students to listen to him more seriously by playing the role of elderly sage.

Young people, he has found, don't pay much attention to someone near their own age. But, though aware of his identity, they listen carefully to the character he has created, Dr. Henry Jacobson.

Mr. Balistrieri gives one-man shows, entitled, "No One Listens Anymore," before groups of students. He dresses in an old Salvation Army suit, with makeup, spectacles, cane and glued-on beard. As "Dr. Jacobson, retired psychologist," he teaches his audience the art of listening.

Young people come into his office, he says, saying they "don't know what to do with their lives . . . but they never looked at themselves to discover what they want. That's where listening comes in—to yourself and to other people."

To really listen to ourselves and to others we have to ignore the masks most of us wear.

"Hear and understand."   [MATTHEW 15:11]

æ   Father, may we listen for Your voice in ourselves and in other people.

THE GRAFFITI ON THE WALLS of one tenement in New York City are different from most. They're about love.

The residents write them, women who live by choice below the poverty level in a Hell's Kitchen walk-up. One says: "Love and never count the cost."

Four nursing Sisters reexamined their vows and decided that the life of Francis of Assisi was timely for them—literally.

Rejecting comforts, they court the lost and forgotten— the "shopping bag ladies," homeless women who often live in doorways or subway stations. They take only $9,000 of their combined salaries at St. Clare's Hospital, sleep on pallets on the floor and rise early to pray together.

At the Dwelling Place, as their refuge is known, they clothe, feed and provide beds for the women with donated food, castoffs and volunteer help.

"One night," says Sister Regina, "one of the ladies was babbling to herself. Another said, 'Hey, no matter what you're talking about, we love you.'"

That's what it all comes down to, doesn't it?

> "Better a dinner of herbs where love is than a fatted ox and hatred with it."
>
> [PROVERBS 15:17]

ĕ₂ Help us to realize, Jesus, that You meant just what You said about love.

UNLIKELY PEOPLE SPOKE UP in behalf of Jesus on Good Friday during His passion and death.

One was Pontius Pilate's wife who, being married to the Roman governor, was herself a pagan. "While he (Pilate) was sitting on the judgment seat, his wife sent word to him, 'Have nothing to do with that righteous man, for I have suffered much over Him today in a dream.'" [MATTHEW 27:19]

Another was the Roman centurion, the commander of a company of infantry: "When the centurion saw what had taken place, he praised God, and said, 'Certainly this man was innocent.'" [LUKE 23:47]

Then, too, there was the thief who hung with Jesus on the cross. He rose above his own agony to defend the innocence of the Savior. Then he heard this joyful promise of Christ: "Truly, I say to you, today you will be with Me in paradise." [LUKE 23:43]

Such goodness in persons who might otherwise be considered far from God should spur us to imitate the Lord in loving every human being.

ê Keep me, Lord, from self-righteousness in my dealing with each person I encounter in life.

For Bob and Golden Bristol, forgiving their daughter's murderer led to their traveling from their Michigan home to the California prison where the convicted man is serving a life sentence.

After driving 2,000 miles, the Bristols told a congregation in the prison chapel that they harbored no hatred toward the man who had killed their daughter Diane. Mrs. Bristol said that God had led them to make the trip, even though friends and loved ones could not understand, because "we knew God could make something good out of this pain."

Michael Keeyes, the prisoner who killed the Bristol's daughter, later told his fellow inmates that "people like the Bristols give meaning to the word 'forgiveness.'"

Jesus told us that we must forgive others. Over and over, He stressed the Father's mercy towards us.

When the Apostles asked Jesus to teach them how to pray, His prayer included, "Father . . . forgive us our sins, for we ourselves forgive everyone who is indebted to us." [LUKE 11:4]

ê   Teach us, Lord, how to forgive.

IN CHRIST'S GLORIOUS TRIUMPH over death, sin and despair on Easter Sunday, there is another note which is sometimes overlooked.

That note is peace—a peace which is the fruit of the Savior's victory. It is the peace for which all men long and which surpasses anything that man himself can attain. It is the peace that can begin in this life and last throughout all eternity.

The very first word Our Lord addressed to His apostles after His resurrection was "Peace!" Then, in the very same breath, He assured them that they would be fortified as no others ever were in their task of bringing that peace to all men.

He gave the 12 the breathtaking assurance that behind them was God—Father, Son and Holy Spirit.

Our Lord told them that they were receiving the very same command from Him that He had from the Father.

We, too, have a share in the sublime commission in bringing divine love and truth to all men.

> "Peace be with you. As the Father has sent Me, even so I send you." [JOHN 20:21]

  Risen Christ, permit me also to be an instrument in bringing Your peace to all mankind.

IT TOOK EIGHT MONTHS, but Tiger the cat was reunited with his master and mistress in Dubuque, Iowa, after travelling 250 miles from Wausau, Wisconsin.

Tiger was lost in Wisconsin in June during Tim and Susan Frommelt's summer vacation. The following February, Tiger appeared at the Frommelt home in Iowa, looking sleek and even a little fat. He was pronounced in good health by the local vet.

One question continues to puzzle the cat's owners: How did Tiger cross the Mississippi River? Tiger isn't talking.

The Creator has provided animals with instincts to support their survival. We marvel at them. Humankind is an even more marvelous work of the Creator and our instincts are to serve Him and to return to Him.

All through history, most civilizations have in some way honored a Supreme Being. Whenever we serve another person, we are imitating the Creator.

"Declare His glory among the nations, His marvelous works among all the peoples!"
[1 CHRONICLES 16:24]

ℰℰ   Lord, help me to appreciate Your creatures.

Is PLAY ONLY FOR CHILDREN? Not at all, says Kirby Sams, recreation director at Elmcrest Psychiatric Institute, Middleton, Connecticut.

"Most people think it's acceptable for children to play and adults to compete," he says. "It's good for adults to play, too."

Mr. Sams set up a giant games event called "Playfair" which stressed games with few rules and no scores. He has found that such games provide exercise and improve self-esteem.

"One of the things I'm trying to do," says Mr. Sams, "is to change the philosophy about sports and athletics for people who have gone through Little League and come out with the aggressiveness of competition."

Many people, he feels, are stagnant. "They don't move around so much and their circulation decreases."

As we get older, we can lose our playfulness, a sense that puts us in touch with God, ourselves and others. Competition has its place, but so does play.

"God richly furnishes us with everything to enjoy." [1 TIMOTHY 6:17]

Keep us from taking ourselves too seriously, Lord.

An Inglewood, California, woman found she had a "little car that can do everything"—even swim.

The auto had been abandoned by its owner when it got stuck in sand on the beach at Will Rogers State Park. She left it there. High tide swept in, floating the tiny auto into the waves.

One of the park's lifeguards spotted the car, bobbing out beyond the breakers. With the help of a 300-foot cable and a police tow-truck, the bouyant little auto was hauled ashore and returned to its surprised owner.

That woman was fortunate to get her car back—thanks to good engineering, a lifeguard's sharp eyes and the cooperation of a number of people.

Those who walk away when things get stuck aren't usually that lucky. Unpleasant situations just don't go away—even if we do. Sooner or later, we all have to deal with the consequences of our actions—or inaction. The sooner, the better.

"For each man will have to bear his own load."
[GALATIANS 6:5]

Jesus, may I face—and master—the challenges of each day.

Spotting a tollfree number for runaways to use to call their parents led to a happy Easter.

The 19-year-old boy had dialed 1-800-231-6946, a number now used in 37 states to convey messages from runaway children to their parents. The telephone program is staffed by volunteers, including some grateful runaways who found their way home through the tollfree number.

In a letter of appreciation to national columnist Abigail Van Buren, the grateful youth wrote "because I read in your column about that tollfree number, which allows kids to call to let their parents know they are O.K., I re-established contact with my parents, went home and had the most wonderful Easter of my life."

Stories like this are reminders to parents to "keep the lines open" all the time. We can prevent much of the anguish that causes youngsters to run away by letting them know they can talk freely with us.

> "Do not be afraid, but speak and do not be silent; for I am with You." [ACTS 18:9,10]

> Jesus, teach us to listen with love and to be open to what our children have to say to us.

THE NATIONAL CANCER INSTITUTE has sharpened an important tool—rehabilitation.

"Our new techniques represent a real revolution in the management of the disease," says Lawrence D. Burke, director for rehabilitation. The program's goals reflect hope: restoration of patients to health; psychological restoration; return to work.

Rehabilitation is team work. Joining the medical staff are psychologists, a variety of therapists, dietitians, vocational counselors and social workers. They give patients and families knowledge and courage to handle posthospital care.

The three-year program in one hospital reduced stays by 18 percent and costs by an average $580. The survival rate increased 19 percent.

Who knows how much hope itself contributes to that increased survival rate? Ailments of body and spirit exist everywhere. Your gift of hope to someone—genuine hope—may make a big difference.

> "Hope for good things, for everlasting joy and mercy."   [SIRACH 2:9]

ఆ   Father, may I nourish my own hope with Your word, so I can give it to others.

Two Britons have devised a computer which will "write" Chinese, a language with 4,500 characters in use today.

The two Cambridge University linguists, one a physicist and patent lawyer, had struggled for two years compiling a Chinese-English dictionary. To speed their work, they built a computer model on a kitchen table with the English equivalent of a child's Erector set, some bits of plastic, string and a cardboard tube from a roll of linoleum. It cost $25 and it worked.

A British communications firm bought the rights to the prototype which followed. The machine may be used for scientific and technical work as well as for printing—replacing the prodigious job of hand-setting hundreds of Chinese ideographs.

"I don't think we could have done it if we'd had a lot of money," says the physicist. "Without money, you have to think harder."

It can be annoying when we are faced with an overwhelming difficulty and someone calls it "a challenge." Try treating it as such. You may be surprised.

"Be transformed by the renewal of your mind." [ROMANS 12:12]

❧ Holy Spirit, fill me with hope instead of despair, faith instead of fear.

Youngsters in team sports play more to have a good time than to win, according to a survey of 531 children aged 9 to 11 in football programs. Most said they would rather play on a losing team than warm the bench for a winning one. Unfortunately, half the young players were pressured by parents who scolded them if they didn't play well.

These findings, by physical education researchers Keith Henschen of the University of Utah and Leon Griffin of the University of New Mexico, showed problems in parents' attitudes toward sports for youngsters. The researchers concluded that parents should attend clinics to help them understand the role of sports for their children.

A child who has lost a game or not played well will benefit more from encouragement than from a scolding. Children are growing, developing, learning and they need the help of adults. Give them every chance you can.

"Let the children come to me, do not hinder them; for to such belongs the kingdom of God." [MARK 10:14]

May I remember, Lord, the best way to get respect is to give it.

$\mathcal{S}$OME DO'S AND DON'TS for the office were devised by top executives of both sexes:

IF YOU'RE A MAN:

● Don't make a fuss over a woman's appointment ("our *first* woman supervisor").

● Be as supportive or critical of women as of men.

● Don't single women out, apologizing for swearing or saying "Good morning, gentlemen—and lady."

IF YOU'RE A WOMAN:

● Plan your career and take risks. Ask, "What can I do to get ahead?"

● Speak at least once in each 10-minute group meeting.

● Don't leap up to serve coffee. Don't knit in meetings.

● Don't depend on men for help. Don't tend to think of men as more learned.

Men and women are equal in ability. Some laws and social customs perpetuate the myth of inequality.

Do we try to treat people of either sex equally? It's worth thinking about, praying about, and acting on.

> "There is neither male nor female; for you are all one in Christ Jesus." [GALATIANS 3:28]

    è   Direct us, Holy Spirit to give more than lip service to the basic equality of all people.

hOW DO YOU TURN a troubled work force from conflict to cooperation?

The General Motors assembly plant at North Tarrytown, New York, had once been threatened with abandonment because of high absenteeism and internal discord.

At considerable cost, training teams taught workers, foremen and supervisors the techniques of good communication and problem-solving through direct involvement.

"For 13 years, all a man knew was that he put the bolts on the front bumper," said a labor expert. "Now he knows where he fits into the whole process."

The plant recently won G.M.'s best quality award, and both sides report morale at an all-time high. "That plant," said a union spokesman, "belongs to every man working in it as much as to the plant manager because we were made a part of it."

What a difference communication made in that plant. It can happen anywhere people feel isolated, cut off from a sense of involvement. Is there an area in your life where a little communication could go a long way?

> "Do not refrain from speaking at the crucial time." [SIRACH 4:23]

ℰℰ Lord, may we break down walls of isolation.

WHAT IS PFO? It's not something from outer space, but an organization with its feet on the ground and its heart in the right place. The initials stand for Pros for Oakland.

PFO is a clearinghouse for athletes who want to help children. Members organized a Special Olympics attended by 850 young hopefuls. They also hold basketball clinics and organize street hockey leagues. Directors ask business organizations to donate lunches and T-shirts for children who attend.

"Everybody donates whatever time he can spare," says a founding member. "Every member pays dues of $15 per month. All expenses are paid by the athletes themselves." The city gives an office.

Says Wells Twombly, sports writer for the San Francisco Examiner, "There are some heroes left."

There still are heroes. You can be one. All you have to do is care about somebody enough to do something to help. It sounds simple. It's not always easy. But it sure pays off.

> "Let your light so shine before men, that they may see your good works and give glory to your Father who is in heaven."
>
> [MATTHEW 5:16]

eć Move us, Holy Spirit, to get out of ourselves and into the world where our efforts are needed.

Naomi Uemura is a 35-year-old Japanese man who thrives on personal challenges. He has climbed to the tops of the highest mountains in five continents, taken the longest-known dogsled trip in the world, and traveled the length of the Amazon on a balsa raft.

And he's not finished! His greatest dream is to cross the 1,800-mile barren Antarctic by dogsled.

Are you picturing a great he-man? Naomi Uemura is only 5-feet 4-inches, but wiry. "It takes the concentration of all my ability to do such things," he says. And he's quick to add that safety is foremost in his mind at all times.

If you put your mind to it, what could you do with your native abilities to fulfill your desires? Maybe not climb mountains—but how about scaling personal obstacles?

There are limits to our abilities, to be sure. But are we really sure what they are? Have we sought and achieved the concentration necessary for solid accomplishment? And asked God for vision and energy?

> "The fruit discloses the cultivation of a tree; so the expression of a thought discloses the cultivation of a man's mind." [SIRACH 27:6]

ᑯ See us through the valleys of our life, Jesus, so we may praise You on the mountains.

THE "BIGGEST SURPRISE of his life" came to 11-year-old Justin Kennedy when 33 truckers rolled into his hometown to visit him.

Crippled since birth, Justin is known as the "Hot Wheels Kid" to truckers he chats with over CB radio as they drive through Chillicothe, Texas. The truckers, in a convoy that roared into the tiny town, parked near the Kennedy home and took Justin outside to ride in some of their big rigs. Meanwhile, other convoy members installed a CB base station in Justin's home that will enable him to talk to truckers up to 15 miles away.

"It was the biggest surprise," said Justin afterward. "I used to ask them if they'd sometime come by if they ever had the time."

The basic goodness and generosity of people is astounding, whether you think of visiting the sick or responding to personal or natural calamities.

You have that goodness in you. Do you tap it often?

> "Be imitators of God, as beloved children.
> And walk in love, as Christ loved us."
> [EPHESIANS 5:1]

Father, show us more ways to love one another.

THE MAYOR OF NORWOOD, New Jersey, his wife and 150 townspeople gathered in a ball field one weekend to drop their cigarettes into a basket and set them afire.

The rally was organized by Patricia Harrison, a housewife. Until the rally, she and her husband, who also quit, smoked 60 cigarettes a day.

Also attending the gathering were members of the state chapter of "GASP"—Group Against Smoking Pollution.

As the flames consumed pipes, cigars and cigarettes, cheers rose from the crowd. But the mayor refused to be over-confident. "It's tough," he said. "I'm chewing a lot of gum."

Giving up smoking—or any other health-injuring activity—is a good idea. But it's not easy. That's why banding together is so helpful.

What do you want to do—or stop doing? Look for some like-minded people. You just may get the help you need.

> "It was kind of you to share my troubles."
> [PHILIPPIANS 4:14]

eð Holy Spirit, may we be a source of encouragement for each other.

CARL SFERRAZA, 17, of Bayside, New York, has a talent, and he isn't wasting any time putting it to use.

An avid student of White House history, he began six years ago sculpting four-inch clay figures of all 37 United States Presidents and their First Ladies. So far, he has made three sets of all the presidents. And he has sent several former First Ladies their own likenesses.

Carl, who also collects signatures and recipes, is now working on a book. It's on White House history.

His work was on exhibit in Federal Hall in New York City and was included in a Bicentennial film shown in Philadelphia.

Time. There never seems to be quite enough of it. But you can start early and make every minute count.

"This is the day which the Lord has made; let us rejoice and be glad in it." [PSALM 118:24]

&ε Father, show us how to put time to better use.

ON EASTER AND MOTHER'S DAY, says Bob Meyer there's a regular "wheelchair convoy" in his Yankee Sil versmith Inn.

The Wallingford, Connecticut, innkeeper has a ramp at the entrance and special restroom facilities for wheel chair patrons. There are five-page menus in braille. He wants to make handicapped customers feel welcome. Yet in his restaurant which seats 600, the handicapped com prise only one percent of the business.

"Our only interest," says Mr. Meyer, "is to get people to do things, to help make things easier for the handi capped in every way... My reward is seeing people more comfortable, able to go out and dine and... not require help in reading the menu."

Others are taking the cue. Telephone calls and letters have come in from all over the country.

We shake our heads over the existence of suffering in the world. But there may be at least one act each one of us could perform—now, where we are—to ease that suffer ing somewhat. Imagine the difference.

> "I will comfort them, and give them gladness
> for sorrow." [JEREMIAH 31:13]

eé   Give us the courage and creativity, Lord, to
take the initiative in making a better world.

A YOUNG POET, Jane Seskin, wrote:
"My Aunt Gladys who's eighty
And never been out of Brooklyn
Called my father last week
And said:
'What's this I hear,
Your Jane, she's not a teacher anymore,
She's a writer?
What kind of life is that
For a single girl?
She should be at that school
With the children—it's more normal.
By the way,
Since she isn't working anymore
Do you think she could
Do some errands for me Friday?'"

A person laboring to write might be surprised by the words, "she isn't working anymore." It's a case of thinking in stereotypes and ignoring reality. How often do you and I fall into that trap?

> "Having eyes do you not see, and having ears do you not hear?"   [MARK 8:18]

℘ Father, may I see each person, including myself, as Your child, with all the possibilities that means.

MICHAEL HERBERT DENGLER has requested a legal ruling that his name be changed to number 1069.

Each of the numerals, says the 32-year-old Minnesota man, has a symbolic significance for him. He started his unusual quest when he lived in North Dakota. Twice the courts turned him down.

When Mr. Dengler moved to Minnesota, he opened a checking account as "1069." He had little trouble passing the checks. When questioned he would reply, "Would I write a bad check with a name like this?" But getting the Hennepin County District Court to sanction the switch was something else. He lost again.

"Dehumanization is widespread," declared Judge Donald Barbeau, "and affects our culture like a disease. To allow the use of a number instead of a name would only provide additional nourishment upon which the illness...would feed and grow."

Our humanity needs to be nurtured. One way is to put people first in your decisions. People before things, before schedules, before anything.

> "Let each of you look not only to his own interests, but also to the interests of others."
> [PHILIPPIANS 2:4]

ĉ? Help me, Lord, to regard each person I meet as a unique human being.

IN *The Story of My Life,* Helen Keller wrote of the ways in which her teacher, Annie Sullivan, led her as a child out of the dark world in which her deafness and blindness had imprisoned her.

"I remember the morning that I first asked the meaning of the word, 'love.' This was before I knew many words...(My teacher) tried to kiss me but at that time I did not like to have anyone kiss me except my mother.

"Miss Sullivan put her arm gently round me and spelled into my hand, 'I love Helen.'

"'What is love?' I asked.

"She drew me closer to her and said, 'It is here,' pointing to my heart, whose beats I was conscious of for the first time...'

"'You cannot touch love, but you feel the sweetness that it pours into everything. Without love you would not be happy'..."

How many of us who are sighted and hearing still remain blind and deaf to what love is?

"He who does not love does not know God; for God is love." [1 JOHN 4:8]

ℰ   Lord, help us to understand the power of love.

THE DAY THAT Ken Waters, an art teacher, prepared to leave Eagle Valley School, his students cried.

A state grant awarded to the 28-year-old Colorado man had expired. Dismay in the elementary school was general. "They know they have a friend," one teacher said of Mr. Waters. "There's no such thing as a failure in Kenny's eyes."

School administrator Walt Timm found some limited funds, but he said the students had to do the most to get the teacher back. "If you want this man," Mr. Timm told them, "somebody is going to have to go to bat for him." The children did. They got their parents to raise enough additional money to reach a minimum wage.

For his part, Ken Waters made do by living in his truck for a term. He says he loves the kids.

Most times, the needs of good teachers aren't quite so dramatic. When they need someone to "go to bat" for them, that someone could be you.

"Encourage one another and build one another up." [1 THESSALONIANS 5:11]

ɛʲ Holy Spirit, inspire teachers to inspire youngsters.

PEOPLE CAN ASK SOME pretty strange questions, according to a *Boston Globe* survey of newspaper public service "action lines" around the United States. Here are some:

- How would you estimate the age of a coin that has the date 1797 on it?
- What is the attitude of Las Vegas, Nevada?
- Where does weight go when you lose it?
- Where do the native-born Floridians go to die? In the obituaries, the deceased are born elsewhere.
- Why does the Navy have rear admirals, not front ones?
- This year they didn't send me what I ordered, just like they didn't send me what I ordered last year. Why did they cash my check if they weren't going to send me anything?

People ask all kinds of questions. Some are humorous and some are puzzling. Many times they are signs of learning and growth—like the countless "whys" of children.

Often the questions are from a deep yearning for truth. The truth is a treasure. Don't hoard it. Share it and you can add meaning to lives.

> "Lead me in Your truth and teach me."
> [PSALM 25:5]

ல் God, remind me that You are the meaning that supports truth.

A LIVE-IN LESSON in community relations has the policemen in Riverside, California, taking a second look at their attitudes towards the city's Chicanos.

In a "get-to-know-the-barrio" program, policemen are given the chance to go to a Mexican town to study Spanish for two weeks. Then they live for several days with a family of the 18,000 Chicanos of Riverside.

"A lot of guys think they're going to be with someone who'll cut their throats," says Patrolman Mike Robitzer, the first cop to live with a family. "Somehow we managed to talk about everything from police brutality to life in Mexico."

Said another officer, "We all have these preconceived ideas. Now I'm a little more open-minded."

To be open-minded is a first step in real human growth. We can be open to God's beauty in nature, in works of art, in people. Pray and work for the opportunity to "open up."

> "Therefore I prayed, and understanding was given me." [WISDOM 7:7]

Keep us from being closed, Jesus, to all You say and do in our lives.

THERE ARE 16 BLUMES running an inn in East Hampton, New York.

When Ken Blume retired from the post office in Greenwich, Connecticut, his wife, Melody, spotted an ad for the sale of a 200-year-old house that had been used as an inn. With their life savings and a loan, they bought it. Ken and Melody Blume and their 14 children, aged 6 to 28, became innkeepers.

Mr. Blume, who had moonlighted as a chef, does all the cooking. His wife does the laundry. Sons and daughters, all part owners, are busy making beds, waiting on tables, tending bar, mowing the lawn, etc. Elizabeth, 18, is at the front desk. Four of them quit jobs to join the family venture.

Each family can work together in its own way. For some it may be no more than assuring each other in little ways of love and support. From such roots come individuals who help make a better world.

> "I have derived much joy and comfort from your love." [PHILEMON 1:7]

ᥱᷓ   Help us, Lord, in our human communities, to work with rather than against each other.

COURAGEOUS MOUSE changed a boa constrictor's diet from mice to hotdogs.

"Easer the Squeezer" was a four-foot boa who had lived happily on the mice dropped into his cage at the home of his New Milford, Connecticut, owner. One day a mouse decided to fight back. It attacked and injured Easer.

Easer was so shocked that he stopped eating. His owner gave the starving snake to the New Milford High School nature center, where Lawrence Kerschnar, science department head, changed its diet.

"I needed something easy to handle, solid and nutritional," Mr. Kerschnar said. He chose frankfurters from the school cafeteria. Now, once a week, Easer has a hot dog pushed down his throat.

Like that plucky mouse, we can get results by not always conforming to the expected behavior. There are times when "fighting back" is the only way of resisting evil. The Lord calls us to be peacemakers, not pushovers.

> "Abstain from every form of evil... and may your spirit and soul and body be kept sound and blameless." [1 THESSALONIANS 5:22,23]

ɛ̃   Make us, Lord, more attentive to Your will.

IN ATHENS, GEORGIA, people are growing high-rise gardens.

The idea came from Michael Dillon of Athens. Old tires are stacked in columns six feet high. Rocks are placed inside. A layer of peat and compost is placed in the joints between the tires, and seeds are planted in the compost.

"People can do the same thing all over the world," says Mr. Dillon, "wherever the motor car is. In one area of one square yard you can grow the equivalent of a 70-foot row of vegetables."

It takes a remarkable imagination to find ways of turning a "throwaway" into a means of growing food. Imagination, plus performance.

How many bright ideas do we get that we don't launch bravely into the world? Others may get a lot out of our brainpower—but only if we put it into action.

> "He made for them tongue and eyes; He gave them ears and a mind for thinking."
> [SIRACH 17:6]

ﻉ   Stimulate our thinking, Holy Spirit, and give us a little shove.

KEEPING THE TV TURNED on at Sol Levine's house is energy-consuming—but the energy is furnished by the Levine children.

Mr. Levine of Highland Park, Illinois, invented a bike-generator. His two children pedal it to power a black and white portable set.

"I'd come home and find my two kids immobilized in front of their set and I figured they should be doing something if they wanted to watch it," says Mr. Levine, president of a center devoted to saving energy. "I took their bicycle, made a stand for it in the TV room, hooked it to a car generator and a 12-volt car battery. Now they can feed their television habit with their own energy and the earth's energy is saved by about one barrel of crude oil a year."

Every bit of energy we use is a drain on the earth's resources. If we use this limited stockpile carefully, there's more likely to be enough for all. We can't be thankful and wasteful at the same time.

"Be thankful." [COLOSSIANS 3:15]

Reinforce our desire to use Your gifts of nature, Father, with loving care.

S ENIOR CITIZENS OFTEN are victims of swindlers. High on the list of methods used to steal from the elderly are home repair schemes. Another gimmick is the offer of financial advice. Then suddenly the victim's life savings are gone.

In St. Louis, Police Captain Virgil Kleine and Shirley Kolar, a bank executive, conduct programs to instruct the elderly how to protect themselves. Unfortunately, Captain Kleine says, embezzlers usually are "middle-aged, low-key and very believable."

Many older people are lonely, don't know where to turn for advice. When approached by someone trying to victimize them, they are too embarrassed to express their doubts and so allow themselves to be intimidated by "slick-talkers."

Do you know elderly people who need true friends?

The first thing they need is not advice, but someone who will take a personal interest in them. Besides being of real service, you may also be the beneficiary of their friendship and long experience. Try it.

"I have called you friends."   [JOHN 15:15]

℮ Enlarge our vision, Lord, to take in the whole world and strengthen our hand in reaching to a friend.

Luke McCann and Alan Anspach, forest rangers in the San Francisco area, feel a glow of humility as they show city youngsters the marvels of nature.

"Seeing mountains and forests on TV doesn't let boys and girls know how it feels to be in the wide open spaces that we take for granted!" they say.

Youngsters have been broadening their experience in summer programs conducted by the Catholic Youth Organization. The children visit city libraries and gyms. They tour butcher shops to see how meat is cut. They also take field trips.

Their greatest thrill comes from seeing God's work, that is so often concealed in the city by crowded construction.

Have your children seen the ocean or the stars at night? It is a sight that has been there from the beginning of creation. And it costs nothing, except the effort it takes to lift up one's eyes and give another the same opportunity.

> "You have made heaven...the earth...the seas and all that is in them; and You preserve all of them." [NEHEMIAH 9:6]

Illumine our spirits, Father, so that we can comprehend more of Your beauty and share it.

WITH AFFECTION, WRITER Phyllis Theroux describes her mother as "a great one for acorns and mustard seeds, where all is dark until one day the light reveals what has been going on all the time."

"She never gave a fig whether any of us came home with A's...," writes Ms. Theroux.

"...We regularly trooped home with rotten report cards...muffed chances, knowing that Mother wouldn't hold these things against us. 'Defeat,' she used to say, 'is nothing more than a learning experience.'

"...While always managing to convey to us that there was something very valid and original in each of us," Ms. Theroux goes on, "she stopped short of telling us precisely what it was...She was simply optimistic enough to believe that one day we would know."

To believe that even one person you know has something important and unique within—and to convince him or her—is a step to revitalizing the world. Take it.

"He encircled him, He cared for him, He kept him as the apple of His eye."

[DEUTERONOMY 32:10]

Lord, help us to understand that You have made each one of us special.

VACATION FOR A GROWING number of families is a week or two of study at a favorite college or university.

Cornell Alumni University, a typical pioneer in the education-vacation concept, has 747 adults and 347 youngsters in four one-week sessions. While parents take courses ranging from astronomy to ornithology, youngsters swim and "learn about bugs and wildflowers" under the care of undergraduates majoring in child care.

"This is infinitely better than going to a resort," says one student-grandmother who attended a Cornell study-week with her 3-year-old grandson.

We're usually at our best when we're doing something, and not just loafing around. The horizon is full of new subjects to learn, interesting people to meet, exciting things to do.

But the horizon won't come to us. We have to move toward it. Ask God's help, and take that step. That may be one of the biggest steps in your life.

"Let your heart take courage."

[PSALM 31:24]

ಆ Give us the courage, Lord, to do something different.

PART OF YOU can go on living even after your body has died. More and more people are requesting that some of their organs be given to others who are ill, or for medical research.

In Scandinavia, it is as common for organs to be donated as it is in the United States for blood to be given. If you knew of someone needing blood, you wouldn't hesitate to offer help. Now, after death, one of your organs may be able to save a life.

This is a good deed that must be planned in advance. Men and women carry cards indicating their wish to donate one or more organs at death. A computerized system in St. Louis at Washington University Medical Center's LIFELINE advises who needs specific organs. The service is free. For further information contact Washington University.

Wouldn't it be a source of personal satisfaction for each of us to know that God's gift of life could continue through us even after death?

"You will be enriched in every way for great generosity." [2 CORINTHIANS 9:11]

Make our determination to be lifegiving persons include all and exclude none, Lord.

THE MOST IMPORTANT factor in your child's self-image, says Dr. Thomas Johnson in his book *Guidelines for Discipline,* is what he thinks you think of him. Dr. Johnson also gives these tips:

● Give attention and praise for good behavior.

● Punishment should be swift, reasonable, related to the offense—and absolutely certain to occur.

● Throw out all rules you are unwilling to enforce.

● Don't lecture and don't warn. Youngsters will remember what they think is important to remember.

● Don't feel you have to justify rules, although you should try to explain them.

● Don't expect children to show more self-control than you do.

● Be honest with your youngster—hypocrisy shows.

● Enforce rules you really feel strongly about—no matter what rules other parents have.

In raising children, as in everything else, what we do speaks so much louder than what we say. Pray for the wisdom to bring word and deed together.

> "Let us set an example...for their lives depend upon us."   [JUDITH 8:24]

    Keep us, Lord, from saying one thing and doing another.

ONESTY IS AS BASIC as the air we breathe, the water we drink, the food we eat.

When honesty takes a holiday... lethal gases, poisonous wastes, toxic additives gradually make our air unbreathable, our water undrinkable, and our food inedible.

Honesty affects where we are, what we do and the things we use every day.

When honesty takes a holiday... building codes, fire-safety regulations, quality controls... can't be trusted to keep our houses sound, our public structures safe and our products reliable.

Honesty holds together our nation, our community, and our very families.

When honesty takes a holiday... a President's oath of office, a doctor's Hippocratic oath, a couple's marriage vows... mean little or nothing.

Yet honesty takes a holiday every time one person "bends" the truth a little, looks the other way, "borrows" something from the office, factory or classroom, overcharges a stranger or undercharges a friend, puts convenience, face-saving or money ahead of principle.

Enough of these "holidays" could make our world unlivable. That's what happens... when honesty takes a holiday.

WHILE MOST FARMERS use chain-saws to cut firewood, Vermonter Armand Gauthier used one to start a new art form.

Mr. Gauthier has carved a place for himself in the art world as the master of the chain-saw. Using no other tools, he carves wooden statues up to nine feet tall—quaint figures with grins that seem to resemble his own.

"I can't make no sad faces," he explains, calling the dozens of elfish forms around his farm "my children." Some hold lamps or magazines. Others have ash trays on their heads. The smiling figures have found their way into ski lodges and restaurants from Vermont to Yugoslavia.

Where does "real life" end and "art" begin? Is art a way of living? Aren't we all, in some sense, artists? These are questions worth thinking about as we go through our daily routine. Are there ways by which a little effort could add beauty and warmth to what we do?

> "Ever since the creation of the world His invisible nature . . . has been clearly perceived in the things that have been made." [ROMANS 1:20]

Waken us to the beauties of Your world, Father, and stir us to preserve them.

COLONEL ERIC HEFFERT HAS the world's rarest profession—helping newborn nations as they emerge into independence.

Col. Heffert, retired from British army service in Nigeria, found his calling when Nigeria asked him back to organize celebrations marking its separation from Britain in 1960. Col. Heffert obliged, and went on to arrange other ceremonies as, one by one, nations broke from British empire ties. He recently arranged rituals for Surinam's independence from the Dutch, and did the same for the British Seychelle Islands in the Indian Ocean.

Now in his sixties, Col. Heffert works 18 hours a day giving instructions in everything from which fork to use to how to lower the old flag and raise the new one. As a former military man, he even teaches schoolgirls to march and drills new cabinet ministers in diplomatic courtesies.

Guiding a nation is a job for all its citizens. Each of us has a stake in helping our own country to achieve goals of peace, justice and love.

"He sought the good of his nation."
[1 MACCABEES 14:4]

   Help us to work together for the good of all our citizens.

ONE DAY IN 1950, RANGERS found an orphaned and badly burned bear cub clinging to a charred tree in New Mexico's Lincoln National Forest.

They had him flown to Santa Fe for treatment and a game warden took him home and nursed him to health. The bear eventually went to Washington's National Zoo where he attracted more visitors than any other animal.

He became Smokey Bear, the familiar poster symbol for forest fire prevention. The bear, in a wide-brimmed forest ranger's hat, warns, "Only You Can Prevent Forest Fires."

Smokey, whose image had achieved international recognition, died recently at age 26. He was flown back to New Mexico to be buried at the Smokey Bear Historical Park.

Why all the fuss? Smokey had become a powerful symbol of concern. He had moved a generation of Americans to action.

Each of us stands for something. Think of what certain individuals have come to represent—Clara Barton, Confucius, Dr. Tom Dooley. What do you stand for?

"Lead a life worthy of the calling to which you have been called."   [EPHESIANS 4:1]

≈ Father, may we make a difference in the lives of others because of the way we live our own.

WRITING THEIR OWN OBITUARIES is part of a 3-week course that is helping 150 teenagers in Elk Grove, Illinois, learn about death as a natural part of life.

"The curtain of mystery about death is being rolled back," says psychologist Joe Wellman of Elk Grove High. "The subject is not something that should be swept under the rug."

Mr. Wellman takes students on trips to funeral homes and has morticians visit classes. Classwork includes discussions of such euphemisms as "pass away," "rest with God," and "kick the bucket." A mock wake is conducted, and students discuss reactions to the deaths of an infant, a teenager, a 40-year-old and an 80-year-old.

Students finishing the course look at life differently, says Joe Wellman. "The uncomfortable feelings we have when the subject of death comes up can be removed."

Talking openly about death can help us to clarify our attitudes towards life. An awareness that death is a fact of life can spur us to live each day more fully.

"Lord ... what is the measure of my days; let me know how fleeting my life is!"
[PSALM 39:4]

❧ Help us to understand, Lord, that death is not an end, but a beginning.

IN CALIFORNIA, PARENTS and teachers are cooperating right in the classroom to help youngsters in the first four grades.

The Early Childhood Education program is a massive effort to get all children, rich and poor, off to a good start. It grew out of research findings which showed that 80 percent of a person's intellectual potential is developed by the time the child is eight.

Aiming for a one-to-10 adult-to-pupil ratio, the program calls for deep involvement of parents both as volunteer teaching aides and in planning for their own school's needs.

One school has achieved a one-to-four ratio. The plan, which includes individual progress records, has succeeded beyond all expectation in its first year.

When parents care about their children's education, things start to happen. If you're a parent, how much are you involved? Homework, PTA, school budgets, bond issues—all need your involvement.

> "The beginning of wisdom is the most sincere desire for instruction." [WISDOM 6:17]

℮ Holy Spirit, may we take an active interest in our children's education.

IN A DEMONSTRATION AT the New York office of the State Bank of India, Mrs. Shakunpala Devi amazed onlookers by solving complex math problems in seconds—much faster than the bank's computer.

For almost an hour, the Calcutta woman fired instant answers to questions on powers to the eighth degree (the sum of a number multiplied by itself up to eight times) and on cube roots. When she calculated the cube root of 274,077,577,255,219,853,331,128,661 in just 20 seconds, the crowd broke into cheers.

"Some of the things she's doing are really almost impossible," said computer company president George Kouchavalis.

Mrs. Devi, who has no formal education, said she hoped "to show people that they should rely less on computers and more on their own minds."

No computer ever built can match the human brain. And no mechanism could ever be devised to duplicate the human capacity for loving and caring. Machines can be good. But they'll never replace persons.

"The plans of the mind belong to man."
[PROVERBS 16:1]

ఆ   Give us a greater sensitivity, Father, to the spark of newness in every person we meet.

IN A DRAMATIC RESCUE at sea, a 64-year-old woman "had one chance in a million to be saved." And she got it.

Mrs. Elizabeth Fuller of Port Elizabeth, South Africa, fell from the passenger liner "Windsor Castle" 250 miles off the Angolan coast en route from Great Britain to Cape Town. Mrs. Fuller's absence wasn't discovered for an hour. Only then did the ship turn around to begin searching for her.

Two hours later, Mrs. Fuller was sighted. She had kept afloat in the 65-degree water by doing the breast stroke and floating on her back. It had been "one chance in a million," according to the ship's captain.

Whatever her chances, that lucky passenger wouldn't have survived if she had given up.

We can't know how our efforts will turn out. If we refuse to try, we lose. If we attempt to go on—whether it's healing a quarrel or revitalizing a neighborhood—our story may have a happy ending.

> "Do not throw away your confidence, which has a great reward."   [HEBREWS 10:35]

ɛ̃   Fill us with greater confidence, Holy Spirit, as we meet the decisions of life.

Two POLICE OFFICERS in New York don't measure success by the number of arrests they make—but by the number of people they can keep out of jail.

The two Bronx policemen began a program for drug addicts who wanted to go straight. They try to persuade addicts to admit to crimes they have committed to buy drugs. Then they accompany the defendants to court and explain that the surrender was voluntary. Addicts may then be enrolled in rehabilitation programs.

"It costs the city about $12,000 a year to keep a person in jail," one of the officers observes. "Drug rehabilitation costs about $1,400 and it works in many more cases than people think."

Dealing only with non-violent, small-scale offenders, the two cops have handled hundreds of cases in this manner, and believe that 70 percent have stayed clean.

It takes more than laws and law enforcement to make our society work. It takes people—in government and out—who care about others and are willing to do something about their convictions. Do we?

> "Let justice roll down like waters, and righteousness like an everflowing stream."
>
> [AMOS 5:24]

When we complain about the problems of today's world, Lord, don't let us forget to light candles.

Some New Jersey towns passed a law which subjects parents to fines or jail terms if their child under 18 is convicted of two criminal offenses in a year.

There are those who think such a law is valuable. They feel kids get into trouble when parents don't care and this forces them to get involved or face legal action.

But there are those who think such a law infringes on a youth's right to confidentiality, since his parent is identified. Also, they claim the law avoids the real issue—a need for more youth recreational and vocational programs.

Whatever the long-term effects of the law two things seem certain: youth problems and concerns are being discussed; and parents are being brought into the picture.

With such a good start, there's hope that some solutions can be found. After all, the family is the basic unit of society.

> "Train up a child in the way he should go, and
> when he is old he will not depart from it."
> [PROVERBS 22:6]

ᴇᴇ́ Holy Spirit, guide parents in their challenging role.

Professor Dennis Holloway's ecology-minded students sparked a revolutionary program at the University of Minnesota. As a result, Winona plans to be a totally energy and resource efficient city by the year 2000.

In 1971, Professor Holloway asked 150 students to design an experimental house stressing conservation. The results were combined in a two-story house called Ouroboros South.

Windmill-generated electricity is stored in 58 batteries. Solar energy provides heat and hot water. A Japanese hot-mist shower and water-saving bathtub cuts water use by 75 percent. Human waste water is recycled by bacterial action into fertilizer and pure water for household use. A greenhouse utilizes the compost to grow food.

Academic institutions and local townspeople can be a great team. As one person, what could you do to bring together people for a common purpose?

"Behold how good and pleasant it is when brothers dwell in unity!" [PSALM 133:1]

Make us more aware of mutual needs, Holy Spirit.

A BRIEF VISIT TO the local pub was one fox's way of eluding his pursuers.

A fox hunt was in full cry in Oxfordshire, England, when the wiley fox scrambled onto the roof of the village pub. Slipping down the chimney, the fox ran through the pub and leaped out the back window, leaving behind him some astonished drinkers and confused hunting hounds.

"If ever a fox deserved to get away," said the landlord afterward, "that one did."

Life's problems are harder to elude than the fox found the hunters to be. And the decision to face up to a hard choice is often just as difficult to make as it is to follow through once we've decided.

Sometimes, like the fox, we can get away. More often we may have to recognize that "the only way out is through."

Ask for God's help to be a straight thinker, even if you can't be a fast runner.

> "If any of you lacks wisdom, let him ask God, who gives to all men generously."
>
> [JAMES 1:5]

꿏 If there's anything we need, Lord, it's wisdom. Give us as full a measure as we can use.

THREE NEW YORK CITIZENS TURNED a 92-year-old woman's tragedy into a beautiful experience.

Eugenia Tolmatchoff had just cashed her $170 Social Security check when her purse was snatched. A sanitation worker and a passerby heard her scream for help and chased the purse-snatcher for three blocks. They subdued him and recovered the purse.

Meanwhile, another passerby asked the weeping woman if he could help. Learning of the theft, he took $170 from his pocket and said: "Here, this is yours. Don't upset yourself anymore."

Minutes later, the thief's pursuers returned with purse and money. The grateful woman refused to keep the extra money. She told police that if her unknown benefactor could not be found, she would give the money to her church on Sunday.

An act of assistance is an act of trust. It builds a bond between persons, releases positive energies and results in the spread of goodness. No candle is ever lighted in vain.

> "Do good . . . be rich in good deeds, liberal and generous."   [1 TIMOTHY 6:18]

     Spur us to be bearers of light and warmth, Lord, in a cold, dark world.

If THOMAS JEFFERSON WERE to see the United States 200 years after writing the Declaration of Independence, he'd be shocked by the cynicism here. So says prize winning biographer Dumas Malone.

"He believed in life, liberty, and the pursuit of happiness," the 83-year-old historian said. "He would want to know why people aren't happy. The thing he'd notice most about the country today is the lack of faith, the wide-spread disillusionment and cynicism, said Malone.

"Jefferson inspired people and gave them faith," he said. "That seems to be missing today," according to Dr. Malone, who is the oldest recipient of the Pulitzer Prize.

One person acting alone won't overcome widespread cynicism. But we can make a start. We can be realistic and hopeful ourselves. We can communicate that attitude to others. We can light candles even while others may be cursing the darkness.

> "Seize the hope set before us. We have this as a sure and steadfast anchor of the soul."
> [HEBREWS 6:18,19]

ᥱᑲ Fire us with hope, Lord, based on what You can do once we put our trust in You.

WHEN A STRAY HUNTING bullet paralyzed 15-year-old Ronnie Donato, he found he was not alone.

When residents of Watertown, New York, learned of Ronnie's determination to function despite his paralysis, they pitched in. Civic clubs and supply dealers gave materials. College students built an addition to the Donatos' home for the teenager's respirator and hospital bed.

A motorized wheelchair, an electric typewriter and a portable respirator were all donated. Ronnie now gets daily visits from a public health nurse and will continue school by two-way telephone.

Already adept at typing with a bar held in his teeth, Ronnie plans a career as a sports writer.

One person's courage can call forth the best efforts of many others. What can one person do? Alone, maybe not the whole job. But one person's good influence seldom stops there. It spills over. It challenges. It inspires. It can work wonders. And each of us is one person.

> "Insist . . . that those who have believed in God may be careful to apply themselves to good deeds." [TITUS 3:8]

ἐ Never let us underestimate, Lord, the power for good You have put into the hands and heart of each.

A MAN OF TODAY SUGGESTS that great minds of the past had something to tell our restless society.

"We are an 'escalator' society, always hurrying and scurrying..." says philosophy professor Dr. Jesse Mann of Georgetown University. "We never seem to be able to rest in the present."

The professor advises that we think about the quality of our lives. He reminds us of wisdom going as far back as Aristotle and Socrates:

- Take time out to think.
- Learn to know yourself.
- Do things in moderation.
- Be willing to take risks.
- Learn to accept things you cannot change.
- Let friendship be more prominent, rivalry less so.
- Do more playing, which is the ability to relax.

We may wonder why advice given so long ago seems so appropriate now. Maybe it's because times change and people don't. Now, as ever, our job is to shape our lives, *and* our times.

"But with those who take advice is wisdom."
[PROVERBS 13:10]

Help us, Lord, to live responsibly.

I<small>T TOOK</small> 10 <small>YEARS</small> but Flatonia, Texas, finally got a doctor to replace its one doctor, who died. That replacement was his daughter.

His death left the tiny community of 1,200, 200 miles from the nearest hospital, without a doctor. Residents rode once a week in a rickety van to nearby towns for medical attention. Then Maurice Wilkinson made them an offer. If the town would lend her the money for medical school, she would practice in Flatonia for at least five years.

The town raised over $100,000 through fund drives and festivals. Maurice finished medical school and Flatonia Community Clinic was built, "a dream come true" for Maurice and her x-ray technician husband.

"Dad's death made me acutely aware of the need for medical care in this area," she said. "All I ever considered in medicine was being a country doctor."

Sometimes two needs can be matched and a real solution found. Look for new ways to solve old problems. Your mind is a storehouse and imagination can work wonders.

> "For the inward mind and heart of a man are deep." [PSALM 64:6]

Remind me, Holy Spirit, of the treasures of mind and spirit you have given me.

Rushia West's 21-year dream became reality as 85 worshippers dedicated the West Community Church of East Granby, Connecticut—a church she had paid for and helped build with her own hands.

Mrs. West, granddaughter of slaves, worked since 1955 on the plain, gray church that stands near the tobacco fields where she had labored since 1917.

She first thought of the non-denominational church in 1955. Mrs. West won approval from the local zoning board and developers. And she spent $8,662 of her own money.

Said Mrs. West, "I hope this little baby being born today is not stillborn but may come of age with God's other churches."

If there is a need, chances are God has provided someone to fill it. Maybe you. How do you know?

You probably don't. You decide. You try. You make mistakes. Then, maybe you find out. Your need to fill may be building a church—or a relationship. It could be anything. But it's up to you.

> "I will rebuild its ruins, and I will set it up, that the rest of men may seek the Lord."
>
> [ACTS 15:16]

eð Make us ready for our moment, Jesus, when it comes.

ARGAIN-HUNTING SHOPPERS in Kalamazoo, Michigan, can save money on transportation around the downtown pedestrian mall—if they travel by rickshaw.

Tom Hatcher, a graduate student at Western Michigan University, charges 15 cents for a ride in his specially built rickshaw. He put it together from odds and ends like bicycle wheels, discarded plywood and pine for the frame.

By night it serves as a mobile home for the young entrepreneur who admits that it is hard making ends meet even though veterans' benefits pay for his studies.

But Tom Hatcher has high hopes for the future, starting with a canopy for the rickshaw and a pedal system to drive it.

"Right now, I'm small," he says. "But everybody starts out small."

Hopes and plans. The two are indispensable to reaching goals. Add imagination and hard work, and you've got a combination that will give you a good start on getting where you want to go—even by rickshaw.

> "But this I call to mind, and therefore I have hope: the steadfast love of the Lord never ceases, His mercies never come to an end."
> [LAMENTATIONS 3:21,22]

Show us the value, Christ, of thinking things through.

WHAT WOULD TEENAGERS choose to do if they had only one day to live? That question was asked of 530 young West German students by teacher Guenther Klempnauer.

Over 100 students said they would take drugs or indulge in sex, while 28 said they would commit suicide. A 16-year-old said, "I would blow myself up with a hand grenade in public protest against the middle classes."

But 111 said they would want to prepare for death by putting their lives in order. Typical of these was one 18-year-old girl's answer: "I would like to spend my last evening in church, alone with God, and to thank Him for my full and happy life."

What a great attitude to have at 18! And asking ourselves that question about death is a good way to focus our attention on the things that are really important to us, on the attitudes we guide our lives by.

What *would* you do if you had only one day to live? It's worth some thought.

"Lead a life worthy of the Lord, fully pleasing to Him." [COLOSSIANS 1:10]

Lord, may we live today—and every day—as if it were our last.

THE VILLAGES OF THOMPSON, Illinois, and Milan, Ohio, are celebrating a common bond—watermelons.

Each community has a watermelon festival on Labor Day weekend. So Thompson, population 600, decided to make the 2,000 residents of Milan honorary citizens. And the people of Milan have reciprocated.

Thompson Village President Fay Ashby said that any Milan resident who visits during the festival will be a guest for all the events and activities there. They will also have a guided tour of the area. Ms. Ashby also sent Milan Mayor Robert Bickly a watermelon plant.

Mr. Bickly noted that it was nice to be a citizen of two communities. And he added, "We hope they enjoy their festival as much as we enjoy ours."

Bringing people together can be as complicated as a SALT treaty or as simple as a watermelon festival. The thing to keep in mind is that the effort starts with one person's decision to build bridges.

That person could be you.

> "There shall be a sowing of peace; the vine shall yield its fruit, and the ground shall give its increase, and the heavens shall give their due. [ZECHARIAH 8:12]

€² Holy Spirit, show us ways to be agents of Divine peace.

THE BULLETIN OF THE COUNCIL for Basic Education has published a list of ways that parents can help children to get a good education. It includes these:

1. Read to your young child as often as possible.
2. Talk regularly with your child's teacher about what can be done at home to support the school's efforts.
3. Insist that your child be home at a reasonable hour and spend a certain amount of time studying each night.
4. Help your child to write fluently. Urge him or her to write a little every day.
5. Encourage your child to speak up on things which are important to him or her.
6. Create opportunities for your child to gain enriching experience outside the classroom.
7. Take your child to the library frequently or encourage him or her to go.

Give a child joy in learning. It's a gift that grows through a lifetime.

> "An educated man knows many things, and one with much experience will speak with understanding." [SIRACH 34:9]

Jesus, may young people learn from us the joy of following Your way.

G EORGE HENNECKE of Closter, New Jersey, is an auto mechanic with a green thumb.

Mr. Hennecke, who manages a gas station, has been a mechanic for over 35 years. When the oil company told him to stop repair and service work and concentrate on pumping gas, he had time on his hands.

"I was going stir crazy," says the station manager. The empty display shelves gave him an idea. "I started bringing a few plants from home and put a few flats of seeds under the fluorescent lights."

The plants flourished: cacti and asparagus fern, rubber and snake plants, figs and peanuts. He has even grown a five-foot lemon tree from a seed.

Customers now bring their ailing plants to Mr. Hennecke to "cure." They swap plants and ask advice. George Hennecke has become a plant "mechanic."

A change that we don't like enters our life: We can fight it, complain. Or—we can look around for new possibilities. A change can be a nudge towards new life. Go with it.

"The law of the Spirit of life in Christ Jesus has set me free." [ROMANS 8:2]

ċᴈ   Help us, Lord, to live creatively.

IN A SENSE, Barry and Suzi Kaufman twice gave life to their son.

A year and a half after his birth, doctors told the Kaufmans that little Raun was autistic. The condition is one of severe withdrawal. Often such persons are institutionalized.

Rather than accept defeat, Raun's parents decided to try to bring their little son "to life."

There followed months of almost constant loving attention and play, marked by acceptance of the child as he was. Communication grew. At four and a half, Raun is ready for kindergarten.

"What we did with Raun," claims Barry Kaufman, "can be used by other people in other situations."

"If people trust themselves," says Suzi Kaufman, "they can do great things."

Love means many things. One of them is acceptance of people as they are. Such acceptance gives them courage—and room—to grow to be what they can be. We could start with the person nearest us.

"Fear not, for I am with you." [ISAIAH 43:5]

ẽ May we love enough, Lord, to work with other people as they are.

EXECUTIVES' DIGEST HAS PUBLISHED some thoughts about winners and losers that are worth thinking about:

"The winner is always a part of the answer; the loser is always a part of the problem.

"The winner says, 'Let me do it for you;' the loser says, 'That's not my job.'

"The winner sees an answer for every problem; the loser sees a problem in every answer.

"The winner sees a green near every sand trap; the loser sees two or three sand traps near every green.

"The winner says, 'It may be difficult but it's possible'; the loser says, 'It may be possible but it's too difficult.'"

You can't "win 'em all." But you can choose to be a winner rather than a loser. A winner accepts defeat, gets up and goes on.

The difference is in attitude. And we're not stuck with our attitudes. We learned them; we can "unlearn" them. "It may be difficult, but it's possible."

> "Straining forward to what lies ahead, I press on toward the goal." [PHILIPPIANS 3:13,14]

℮ Help us to understand, Jesus, that in losing You won.

A MICHIGAN WOMAN READ a series of newspaper ads which changed her life.

Sister Rosemary Havey, a 41-year-old teacher, had master's degrees in both chemistry and biology. The ads she saw were for medical help. "Not Africa, not China— but county after county without doctors right here in my native Michigan." She made her decision.

She got her M.D. and opened practice in the tiny town of Sebewaing in northern Michigan. The heavily Protestant community, population 3,000, welcomed her and two sister assistants with open arms.

The town converted a former bank into a clinic. The fire department helped them move in. Her parish equipped her car with a citizens' band radio.

"I became conscious of an unfulfilled need," says Dr. Havey, "and I did something about it."

Many of us are not even aware of the needs around us. Even when we are, sometimes we figure that someone else will take care of them. Maybe you are "someone else."

> "Let no one seek his own good, but the good of his neighbor." [1 CORINTHIANS 10:24]

ಆ May I remember, Father, that we are brothers and sisters, and that we need each other.

WANT TO HOLD AN AUDIENCE spellbound? Vince Vinci in *Meetings and Conventions* magazine gives four basic steps to aspiring speechmakers:

- Know them. Glance over your audience. Are they young, old, affluent, poor? Are they a group with a special interest? Talk to them as individuals.
- Think big. Keep gestures big, pictorial. Don't shy away from forceful, dramatic expression.
- Tap their memories, experiences, senses. Don't say "house" when "grey, weather-beaten cottage" will put them right at the edge of the picture.
- Give loving care to the organization of your speech. Tell them what you are going to say. Say it. Tell them what you have said. Repeat. Connect. Emphasize. And keep it constantly alive and tied together.

Spellbinders are probably born, not made. But steps like these can make any of us better communicators. And don't forget to give loving care to the people to whom you're talking. That's one message everybody wants.

> "To make an apt answer is a joy to a man, and a word in season, how good it is!"
>
> [PROVERBS 15:23]

∞ May we be more ready to share with others, Father, whatever You've given to us.

IN MALI, ON THE BANKS of the Niger River, the world's largest solar power plant will soon whirr into motion.

Jean-Pierre Girardier's solution to high prices of oil and of servicing remotely located machinery is his solar engine designed for such places. The French government is financing the $1,000,000 plant he is building.

His partners for the project, greater than anything yet powered by the sun, include the French Atomic Energy Commission and the French Petroleum Company.

Every day, the solar power station will pump enough water from the Niger to irrigate 37 acres of land, supply drinking water for up to 10,000 persons, refrigerate a cold-room for an agricultural co-operative, generate power to light the co-operative and a 40-room hotel.

The vast power of the sun is a reminder of the resources available to us in personal need. There is strength deep within us derived from God's unlimited power. He is there waiting to be sought.

> "This is the confidence which we have in Him, that if we ask anything according to His will He hears us." [1 JOHN 5:14]

ဆ Holy Spirit, help us to realize we have only to ask.

EVERY PATIENT HAS the right:

1. to considerate and respectful care;

2. to complete information about his diagnosis, treatment and prognosis;

3. except in emergencies, to full information before giving consent to a treatment;

4. to refuse treatment to the extent permitted by law;

5. to privacy concerning his medical care program;

6. to confidentiality of medical records;

7. to evaluation, service and/or referral;

8. to know the relationship between his hospital and other institutions;

9. to continuity of care;

10. to have all items of the bill explained;

11. to know which hospital regulations apply to him as a patient. (American Hospital Association)

As a patient, you have the right to be treated as a mature, responsible adult.

> "In everything a prudent man acts with knowledge." [PROVERBS 13:16]

℘ Make us aware of our responsibilities, Holy Spirit, and of our rights.

MAINE'S PROJECT INDEPENDENCE HAS shown what any teenager knows—that "wheels" make a difference.

When a 1970 survey by the state's Committee on Aging revealed that senior citizens in Androscoggin, Franklin and Oxford counties were isolated, ill and undernourished, a fleet of minibuses was formed.

Called Project Independence, it transports the elderly, free of charge, to doctors' and dentists' offices, banks, social events and meal sites. In one year, the Project's buses covered 250,000 miles, serving 60,000 riders.

Project Independence is one of hundreds of similar efforts to give older persons more mobility. If your community has such a program, maybe you could volunteer. If it doesn't, you might furnish the spark that could start things going. Why not? After all, you may one day need it yourself.

> "Let not your hand be extended to receive, but withdrawn when it is time to repay."
> [SIRACH 4:31]

Holy Spirit, may we reach out to all in our community.

HIGH SCHOOL GRADUATION with honors was more than just a proud occasion for Susan Forman and her parents. It was a tribute to a great deal of love and hard work. Susan is totally deaf.

"I was exposed to rubella when I was one month pregnant," recalled Mrs. David Forman after Susan's graduation from New York's Canarsie High School. "We wanted children. We hoped for the best."

Diagnosed totally deaf at age 18 months, Susan began years of training at the New York League for the Hard of Hearing. Progress was slow. Each new word had to be pronounced to her thousands of times.

But Susan did learn, and after graduation she returned to the League to speak. Her message to the children there was touchingly brief. She asked them to remember that their parents need a lot of encouragement.

All of us need a lot of encouragement. And our own needs can be clues to opportunities to give it. Who in your life can you think of who would benefit by what you can offer today? There's no better time to do it than now.

> "Let us then pursue what makes for peace and for mutual upbuilding." [ROMANS 14:9]

As we become more sensitive to our needs, Jesus, help us to reach out in love to others.

DAY CARE WORKERS Jimmy Garrett and Derek Culpepper are as big and strong as football halfbacks—and the pre-school youngsters they cared for loved them.

Mr. Garrett and Mr. Culpepper became teachers as part of an experimental two-year program designed by Dr. Boyd McCandless, Emory University sociology professor.

Dr. McCandless feels that the program proves that toddlers need fathering as well as mothering.

The project employed 13 males to work in several Atlanta day-care centers with pre-schoolers. Said one center director: "It most definitely helps to have men around. Men never yell. Men are more apt to tolerate diversity of behavior."

Dr. McCandless found that youngsters became more trusting, and able to respond to displays of warmth from both men and women.

It may come as a surprise to learn that men work in day-care centers—until you think about it. So it goes with many of the roles set by custom. Often it pays to say "why?" and then "why not?"

> "And it is my prayer that your love may abound more and more, with knowledge and all discernment." [PHILIPPIANS 1:9]

 Assist us, Holy Spirit, to think clearly, act boldly and love generously.

A Santa Barbara reader wrote to tell us what happened after she wrote to a company she'd had problems with:

"About that time I was entertaining a friend from Chicago... We were stranded at the University of California campus one rainy day, and the cab dispatcher said he couldn't send a cab that far."

She knew the owner of the cab company had already ignored appeals in the press for better service, so she wrote to the new manager of the company.

"A few days later," she wrote, "the man knocked at my door to tell me, 'thank you.'" He had found such a deluge of complaints awaiting him in his new job that he felt he was too old to face it and decided to retire. Her letter changed his mind. He and a fellow driver would buy the company and start fresh.

They have been operating successfully ever since.

The tone of a letter is as important as a smile in a conversation. Present criticism constructively, perhaps with a concrete alternative. Your points will be more effective when you are courteous.

> "Show perfect courtesy toward all men."
> [TITUS 3:2]

  May I love my neighbor, Lord, in all the situations in my life.

JIM SEAVER IS A LOOKOUT for forest fires.

He spends his winters in a log cabin, and his summers in a five-by-five-foot cubicle on top of a seven-story tower. He is alone much of the time. Mr. Seaver keeps busy by reading, playing his banjo and tending his two cats.

Jim Seaver is one of a dying breed. More and more, surveillance aircraft are being used to patrol forests. So spotters are being phased out in national forests and most states. He'll miss it, Mr. Seaver says. He likes his job and finds it a source of contentment, not boredom.

Some people love to be alone. But for many—and occasionally for all of us—being alone means being lonely, a painful, unpleasant experience.

Do you know someone who's alone? An older person or invalid? Make a phone call, drop a line, pay a visit. You'll make two lives richer if you do.

> "Bear one another's burdens."
> [GALATIANS 6:2]

ᶜᵉ   Jesus, may we reach out to each other in our times of loneliness.

T EENAGERS THEMSELVES WANT a high school diploma to be proof of real educational attainment, according to a Gallup Youth Survey.

When questioned, 63 percent of the students polled said they favor a proposal requiring all high school students to pass a nationwide examination before receiving their high school diplomas. Of adults questioned on the issue, 65 percent approved the proposal.

One teenager expressed the views of many, saying, "I don't know who they think they're kidding by letting kids graduate from high school who can barely read or write. They're only putting off the problem. Wait till these kids have to cope with the adult world and find out they can't."

That teenager has very aptly summed up a sound attitude: There's no "free lunch." Postponing a problem doesn't solve it. It just delays facing the inevitable consequences of our decisions. How do you handle the problems in your life?

> "Because you have asked . . . for yourself understanding to discern what is right, behold, I now do according to your word, behold, I give you a wise and discerning mind."
>
> [1 KINGS 3:11,12]

Lord, move us to seek constructive solutions.

ROUGHLY 2,500 COUPLES RALLY annually in Hempstead, New York, to celebrate happy marriages.

The celebrants are among 150,000 couples in the Marriage Encounter movement which began, in this country, in 1968. It aims to help people in good marriages make them better, largely through better communication and shared spirituality.

Those involved have all made a special weekend retreat. It focuses on an honest and deeply personal appraisal of themselves and their marriage.

A leader gives the couples key questions to talk over alone. One, for instance, could be, "What three small things most united you?" Says one woman, "It puts you back into the romantic stage, where you were when you were first married."

Individuals develop their attitudes and the ways in which they will live with other people in the family. By the example of a mature relationship, parents can sow the seeds of future good marriages.

> "...that their hearts may be encouraged as they are knit together in love."
>
> [COLOSSIANS 2:2]

    Help us, Lord, to realize that it is the way we live that teaches more certainly than what we say.

CLARE BOOTHE LUCE HAS HAD a busy life as actress, journalist, playwright, congresswoman from Connecticut, ambassador to Italy and lecturer.

In an interview for *People* magazine, she was asked if she had any regrets.

"Yes," she said. ". . . Sometimes I wake up in the middle of the night and I remember there was a girlhood friend of mine who had a brain tumor and called me three times to come and see her."

"I was always too busy," Mrs. Luce goes on, "and when she died I was profoundly ashamed. I remember that after 56 years."

It happens to all of us: The request for a bit of our time—an interruption of plans, an assault on routine. We're too busy. Is "too busy" a matter of the things we have to do, or of choices we make?

Next time it happens ask the question: "What is the best use of my time?" Choose thoughtfully. Choose with love. There'll be no regrets.

"What do you want me to do for you?"
[MATTHEW 20:32]

eé May we see You, Jesus, in the moment when someone in need asks for our time.

A COLLEAGUE TELLS A STORY about a Nobel Prize winner in physics.

Dr. John Hasbrouck Van Vleck, of Harvard, considered by some the "father of modern magnetism," knows many, perhaps most, of the railroad timetables of this country and Europe.

"He can tell you instantly how to get from one place to another by train," says the colleague. He then relates an incident in which a student asked Dr. Van Vleck for a routing and was told to change trains in a certain small Illinois town.

The student checked the timetables. He told the professor he must have been wrong—the first train arrived shortly after the second left. "Yes," the physicist replied, "but that train is always late."

It's refreshing to find a Nobel Laureate who's a railroad buff. That knowledge humanizes one we could easily suspect was dry, dusty and aloof.

It's also a lesson in the foolishness of snap judgments. First impressions are often dead wrong.

> "Hasty judgment has led many astray, and wrong opinion has caused their thoughts to slip." [SIRACH 3:24]

≈ Father, may I not judge by superficial appearances.

EVERY YEAR, ONE BUSY Texas dentist takes a month's vacation in some remote place—and fixes teeth.

Last year it was the mountains of Taiwan. Through the Direct Relief Foundation, Dr. Melvin Land answered the request of a Maryknoll missioner for a dentist to serve among the aborigines there.

After a 24-hour flight and a harrowing ride to the missioner's small compound in a mountain village, Dr. Land set up headquarters. A stream of patients stood at his door the very next morning, and the Dallas dentist was practicing newly-learned words for "open wide, please" in mountain dialects.

For years, Dr. Land had mailed checks to various charities. "But somehow that didn't seem enough . . ." he says. "I began to inquire just how I could help."

Someone once said, "If you care enough to send the very best, send yourself." It's worth thinking about.

> "He delivers the needy when he calls, the poor and him who has no helper. He has pity on the weak and the needy, and saves the lives of the needy." [PSALM 72:12,13]

Father, all Your needy children are my brothers and sisters. Don't let me forget it.

ᕼERE, ACCORDING TO the *Successful Supervisor*, are some ways to dodge a decision:

1. Take flight into detail.
2. Delegate the problem to a committee.
3. Look for the answer in the "book."
4. Induce the boss to commit himself on how to handle the problem.
5. Give an answer in doubletalk.
6. Delegate the problem to a subordinate.
7. Have a study made to "get all the facts."
8. Call in an expert to "make sure we're on solid ground."
9. Deny that any problem exists.
10. State that the problem belongs in someone else's province.
11. Counsel infinite delay of action.
12. Simply put on your hat and go home.

The responsible course of action is to use our ingenuity in solving problems rather than in dodging them. How do you face problems?

"A man's mind plans his way."

[PROVERBS 16:9]

℮ᵌ Give me the wisdom, Lord, to make good decisions.

For Richmond, Virginia, residents, cancer facts are now as close as the nearest telephone.

Through a program developed at the Medical College of Virginia, there are 86 tapes available to callers. Some—on subjects like chemotherapy and radiation side effects are available only by doctor's prescription. Others are available on request.

The information, recorded in non-technical terms, is intended to encourage early diagnosis of cancer, and to remove the aura of fear surrounding the disease. Callers who want to discuss their problems with someone are referred to individuals in the cancer center at the college.

Good communication—clear, accurate and non-technical—can have many healing effects.

Are you a good communicator? Do you know what you are talking about? Can you organize your material clearly without oversimplifying? Do you really want to get something across?

If so, there's a lot of good you can do.

"The mind of the righteous ponders how to answer."   [PROVERBS 15:28]

❧ Help us sharpen our skills in communicating, Lord, in a world of confused messages.

Tips for energy conservation can apply to our bodies as well as our cars and furnaces, says one physician. He listed these points for conserving our bodies as "nonrenewable resources":

● Check your present power plant. Make sure it's functioning efficiently. A malfunctioning heart or liver will waste your body's energy.

● Take it easy. Worrying or rushing is like spinning your wheels—and results only in lost vigor.

● "Insulate your attic." Thought, planning and study are the insulation the human cranium needs to prevent mistakes and wasteful, unworkable schemes. Conservation, says the doctor, can mean not only a longer life, but a better one.

It's laudable to want to preserve and enrich the physical environment. But let's not forget the more personal "nonrenewable resources." After all, we are made in God's image. Shouldn't we act that way?

"I pray that all may go well with you and that you may be in health."   [3 JOHN 1:2]

Father, may we value the works of Your hands—starting with ourselves.

PARISHIONERS OF ST. PHILIP'S CHURCH in Columbus, Ohio, heard an unusual appeal at mass one Sunday morning.

Father Richard Engle expressed his concern about several attempts made on the life of former President Ford. He urged owners of handguns to turn them in the following Sunday.

The results were revealing: Twelve handguns, 16 starter pistols and 20 toy weapons were turned in the next week. The metal was melted down and made into crosses.

"This is saying an awful lot about how sick our society is," said the priest. "I don't think the answer is to go out and buy more guns."

Violence comes at us from every direction—the media, personal relations, even the family. The way to respond—Christ's way—is to try to act in a non-violent manner.

Our attempt to avoid and reduce violence can be a following of Jesus, whose message was peace.

> "Mend your ways... live in peace, and the God of love and peace will be with you."
>
> [2 CORINTHIANS 13:11]

Grant us the strength, Lord, to sow love where there is hatred.

CUSTOMERS WHO GO TO Curtis Little's barbershop may get a sermon with their haircut or pastoral counseling with their shave. Mr. Little is a 53-year-old Evangelist minister. He considers his Hackensack, New Jersey, barbershop his parish.

Mr. Little, a barber for 20 years, also officiates at weddings, funerals, christenings and baptisms.

He says, "I feel I can reach the people better as a barber . . . I've found many who need to tell their problems to someone. My work as barber, minister and evangelist all fit in well together. I'm able to make my own livelihood rather than depend on contributions." Mr. Little explained that his father was a barber, his uncle a minister. He feels that he has been able to combine the two in a satisfying career.

St. Paul made his living as a tentmaker, so a clergyman with another job is an idea with a long history.

Each of us can minister to others if we have a listening heart, good judgment and a will to care.

"See that you fulfill the ministry which you have received in the Lord."

[COLOSSIANS 4:17]

Increase our sense of responsibility, Jesus, for the people who are part of our lives.

CHILDREN HIT THE NAIL on the head during a strike by apartment house workers in New York City.

One day the tenants' committee in a Greenwich Village high-rise posted a sign in the building's automatic elevator. It read:

"Please be very careful when using the elevators as they cannot be repaired for the duration of the strike if they break down. Parents, please prevent children from playing with the controls."

A day or two later another sign appeared, just below the first one. It was written in a scrawly hand.

"Adults: Please settle your disagreements.

THE CHILDREN"

The children certainly had a point. Yet the solution to such disputes is never simple.

What can we do about it? Can we increase the amount of harmony around us? Cut down the discord? How? We could try, where we are, to go the extra mile for one other person. It would be a start.

"Men, you are brethren, why do you wrong each other?" [ACTS 7:26]

✍ You gave us the solution, Jesus. May we have the courage to live Your way.

IN A LETTER TO *The New York Times,* James Smith of Dumont, New Jersey, had this to say:

"For years I was a 'do-gooder.' It was good for my ego. However, I found that it was no longer 'in'... so I drifted with the crowd who moans and groans and does nothing but point the finger of success at the poor.

"Well, things have changed... I have come to realize that it is indeed a great blessing to be able to help in any small way to touch those who suffer...

"There is a place in the city called 'Under 21'... Here you will see people who work with young street kids, nomads and runaways. In trying to help these kids to find a new beginning, I am finding a new beginning.

"There are two rules that are necessary for 'success' at Under 21. I must try very hard to love these kids. I must pray a lot..."

When you really care, your efforts bring the warmth of your love to others. And prayer helps, too.

"Love one another earnestly from the heart."
(1 PETER 1:22)

Help us, Jesus, to care as You did, by sharing the suffering of others.

IN Virginia, A 65TH birthday opens the door to a whole new world in 39 colleges and universities.

A state law gives Virginians 65 and over a chance to take adult education courses free in all the state's public institutions of higher learning. If their incomes are under $5,000 yearly they may also enroll in full-credit courses free. For those over the $5,000 income level, tuition is half-price.

Although many universities in other states give reduced or free tuition to senior citizens, Virginia lawmakers believe theirs is the first law providing a state-wide plan for involving the elderly in its total college program.

What a great idea . . . to make state-funded colleges and universities serve the retirement needs of older citizens. There's no reason why every state in the Union couldn't have such a law. No reason, except that so few of us have asked for it. How about asking?

> "Ask, and you will receive, that your joy may be full." [JOHN 16:24]

⊷ Jesus, may we be innovative in serving the needs of the people.

ARE YOU READY for developments like these:

• In the future, words printed on paper will cease to be our chief means of recording and storing information. Computers will replace filing cabinets.

• Telecommunications will cut the need for business travel and even for commuting.

• TV viewers will have a wider range of choices giving them much greater control over what they watch.

• Home communication units may be part TV set, part telephone and part mailbox. They will be linked with the household computers.

• Home video units will join households with people, institutions and computers anywhere in the world, making available all accumulated knowledge.

With such access to knowledge, says Gene Roddenberry, creator of Star Trek, "barriers will begin to crumble."

Try other ways to make barriers crumble—now. Listen more. Consider someone else's ideas. Be able to say, "You're right." Communication, after all, is between people. And we're all people.

> "Hear the commandments of life . . . give ear, and learn wisdom." [BARUCH 3:9]

Help me, Lord, to be really open to what others are trying to say.

THE AMERICAN REVOLUTION was over more than 50 years when the Japanese first heard about it.

A 17th century Japanese edict had virtually cut off the country from foreign lands for security reasons. Only the Dutch had some limited contact.

In 1826, an astrologer heard from the Dutch of the existence of the United States. Only in 1853, when Commodore Perry arrived, did Japan grasp its significance.

Sixteen years later, Yukichi Fukuzawa, founder of Japan's oldest university, wrote a book on the West containing a translation of the Declaration of Independence. He put our concept of equality this way: "Nature does not produce man above man, nor does it produce man beneath man."

That translation of "all men are created equal," sharpens a familiar truth. But note: "created" is missing. Our founders believed in a Creator Who gives us our rights—and calls us to brotherhood. And that makes all the difference.

"He who loves his brother abides in the light, and in it there is no cause for stumbling."
[1 JOHN 2:10]

Father, help us remember what we share as Your children, rather than what divides us.

SEVERE PHYSICAL HANDICAPS no longer mean lifelong dependency for quadriplegics in Columbus, Ohio.

Creative Living, a housing venture, is the only privately owned residence in the United States designed for the chairbound person with restricted arm movements. Its 18 units have pressure-activated doors, specially placed storage space and electrical outlets. Ohio State University students work as attendants.

Creative Living residents have shown that they are mentally independent. Rather than medical supervision, what they really need is a paid staff assistant around the clock. Many have begun furthering their education and even preparing for careers.

The handicapped can often go farther than we might think in developing independence and self-mastery. If external circumstances are favorable, their inner drive can get a big boost. What is being done for the handicapped in your community? Is more needed? Where do you fit in?

> "Let each of us please his neighbor for his good."　　　　　　　　　[ROMANS 15:2]

❦　Teach us, Jesus, to remember those with special needs.

IN Rome, GEORGIA, no student's education is complete without some first-hand work experience.

The city's school system has a unique job placement service for any student of employment age. Students work during summers and after school in factories, business offices, stores and government agencies. In one year, over 500 students found placements.

"If a student hasn't held a job or been exposed to the world of work by the time he graduates," says Mary Huckaby of Rome's job placement program, "he's going to find a whole different world out there."

Another aim of the program is to help develop positive attitudes about work and job responsibility.

"Our employers say that most students do a good day's work for a day's pay," says Mrs. Huckaby, who sees the service as a real success.

There's more to life than working. And there's more to work than casual drifting into something that pays. What are you doing with your life? What do you want to do? It's up to you.

> "Trust in the Lord and do good ... and He will give you the desires of your heart."
>
> [PSALM 37:3,4]

  Make us more thoughtful, Lord, about the work we do—and ready to do it better.

WOULD A YOUNG William Shakespeare trying to sell his plays today have a tough time? G. Wilson Knight, a leading Shakespearean critic, thinks so.

"Shakespeare's point of view is not one which is easily accepted today," says Mr. Knight, author of eight books about Shakespeare including, *The Wheel of Fire*.

"He has a kind of faith in human nature. He's also not a defeatist writer. True there are many evils in the plays and much suffering, but . . . on the whole the plays are optimistic." His writings weren't filled with a lot of denegation, criticism, and cynicism "which we take for granted today," says Mr. Knight.

Faith in human nature, beginning with our own, may not always be in style, but it is a time-tested way to lead a life that has value.

Shakespeare will outlive the negative attitude found in so many areas today. And so will our efforts, if we place our trust in God, ourselves and the basic goodness He has given all people.

"You, O Lord, are my hope, my trust."
[PSALM 71:5]

    Give us a viewpoint, Holy Spirit, that is realistic but intensely hopeful.

AFTER THEIR FATHER DIED of cancer, teenagers Keith and Kevin Rossignol took over his contracting business and built their family a $50,000 home.

There was no money left after their dad's terminal illness wiped out the family savings. But the 17-year-old twins determined to save their father's business by doing the work themselves. Working nights and weekends, the brothers completed high school, ran the business and built a home for their mother and younger brother in Chittenango, New York.

"He had this dream about us staying together," Keith explained. "Our dad taught us everything he knew. He started with nothing."

Says a friend of their father, "What these two have done is not something you take for granted about kids their age. They did this on their own."

A parent's legacy can be found in his or her children. Much of what fathers and mothers do is an act of faith in the future as much as for the here and now.

> "I know the plans I have for you, says the Lord, plans for welfare and not for evil."
>
> [JEREMIAH 29:11]

Father, give parents a steady sense of hope in each other, their children and in You.

WHEN YOU GIVE INSTRUCTIONS, in your office, your home, your classroom or anywhere else, are you dissatisfied with the results?

It's possible the fault is yours. *Executives' Digest* lists some common errors:

1. *Taking understanding for granted.* Watch for signs of confusion or hesitation. In such cases, explain in different words what you want.

2. *Expressing orders negatively.* Telling people what not to do is confusing. Be positive.

3. *Speaking unintelligibly.* Some people feel uncomfortable telling other people what to do. They blurt it out or mumble and take off, leaving the other person to figure out what they said. Speak clearly.

4. *Giving too many orders at once.* Trying to cover too much ground may result in nothing being accomplished. Take things one at a time.

How we speak to people has a lot to do with how well our authority is heeded. To speak with understanding, clarity and love is to speak volumes.

> "On the lips of him who has understanding wisdom is found." [PROVERBS 10:13]

ℰℒ Guide us, Jesus, to follow Your way of communicating with others—with respect and love.

MILLIONS ARE HUNGRY and their hunger is daily. One group of women isn't waiting for people in high places to take action.

The 1,600 Sisters of Charity of the Blessed Virgin Mary have pledged part of their annual income to a BVM Hunger Fund—over $50,000 in two years.

Funds have gone to a feeding and nutrition-education project in Calcutta; an agricultural training program in the Dominican Republic; a well-digging project in India; a demonstration garden in Senegal.

"This money comes from each sister's personal budget," a spokeswoman explained. "An average of $20 per sister."

"It relates us to the parable of the Widow's Mite," she says, "and to the poor with whom we vow to cast our lot."

We can be overwhelmed by the staggering numbers of people in need and say, "What can I do?" Or we can try to picture just one man, woman or child. And try to make life more bearable for that person.

"I would give my bread to the hungry and my clothing to the naked." [TOBIT 1:17]

୧ Father, help me to feel deeply the need of my brothers and sisters.

ЄACH JULY, NANAIMO, British Columbia, hosts the world's most ridiculous boat race—the great International Bathtub Race.

Up to 300 entries come from such countries as Australia, Mexico, the United States and Great Britain. The bathtubs may be powered by sails, paddles or engines. Pontoon tubs, outrigger tubs, hydrofoil tubs and even steam-powered, sternwheeler tubs splash across the 35-mile Strait of Georgia to Vancouver. Half sink in the first 10 minutes. Only one in six finishes.

Said one winner, "You get bounced around that cramped bathtub until your legs get numb. The whole race is a battle of trying to keep the tub straight into the swells and bailing out water at the same time."

Tender boats follow the tubs, fishing out hapless racers whose tubs sink.

Racing bathtubs may not be everyone's idea of fun. But maybe we could all use a bit more light-heartedness in our lives. Pick a flower, buy a balloon, kiss a child. Smile. God didn't make us to be gloomy.

"You will have joy and gladness."

[LUKE 1:14]

Jesus, give us the joy that is the Father's promised gift.

WHEN John E. BARTON SENT his reflections on prison life to the *San Francisco Examiner*, he also sent this biographical information:

"I was sentenced to a life term in prison in December, 1943, for the murder of a 19-year-old girl in San Pedro. I was also 19, in the Navy, awaiting a leave home from a tour of duty in the South Pacific as a gunner in an Armed Guard crew on a merchant ship.

"I arrived at San Quentin, January 6, 1944, and was ultimately paroled from the Medical Facility at Vacaville, June 26, 1959. Since being released from prison I have married, have five children, all in school.

"I have finished my education to the extent of a Master's Degree in vocational education, and am currently employed by the State Department of Education in Salem (Oregon) as a curriculum specialist.

"I have received a full and unconditional pardon from Governor Ronald Reagan, June 29, 1968."

Can you help someone to look at the wreckage of his or her past and, on it to build a new life?

> "Those who are well have no need of a physician, but those who are sick . . . I desire mercy, and not sacrifice." [MATTHEW 9:12]

As You prayed, Jesus, help us to forgive—and to help.

HEN OVERDEVELOPMENT threatened to wipe out all the natural wilderness of South Florida, concerned residents of Boca Raton pooled their efforts to preserve one of the few remaining natural areas of its kind— Spanish River Park.

The park is 46 acres of permanently protected public land, bounded by the Atlantic Ocean and the Intercoastal Waterway. Its story began in 1966, when citizens approved a $1.5 million bond issue to develop the site. A planning firm was engaged, another bond issue and a Federal grant completed the project, which by then included 1,850 feet of priceless beachfront.

In 1975, over a million visitors enjoyed the award-winning park, which asks only that all comers "Take nothing but pictures, leave nothing but footprints."

Our country's parks and roadsides are covered with litter because so many of us so often ignore the message of that simple request.

Do you think of the next person when you use a public facility?

> "For from the greatness and beauty of created things comes a corresponding perception of their Creator." [WISDOM 13:5]

God, may my actions show that I am a lover of Your good earth.

Mrs. Perlina Wells has been around for a long time. She's possibly the oldest known resident of Georgia.

The daughter of slaves, Mrs. Wells is estimated to be between 105 and 110 years of age. Like other young black girls after the Civil War, Mrs. Wells tended sheep, goats, and flocks of turkeys and carried water to field hands.

Over the years, Mrs. Wells has come to find comfort in religion. And she says she's sorry that such things didn't concern her in her younger days.

"But now I love the Lord and He loves me. I have never done anybody harm so I don't have a bit of trouble falling to sleep when I go to bed."

That's nice to be able to say after a century of life.

The comfort we find in religion is something that can grow with time. If it deepens and expands, our faith puts us in touch with what is most vital about why we're on earth—to love God above all and our neighbor as ourselves.

"Glory and honor and peace for everyone who does good." [ROMANS 2:10]

Whether our lifespan is long or short, Father, let it be filled with all the good we can cram into it.

WHEN FLOPPY-EARED THURBER first went to work as a canine detective at the Charlottesville-Albemarle County Joint Security Complex, the officers there laughed. They doubted that the sad-eyed bloodhound would even be worth the table scraps fed him.

But Thurber has since proved himself and is now regarded as one of the top sleuths in rural, central Virginia. With his sensitive nose and four legs, he's helped recapture six wanted men and five wanted juveniles, and rescued one child.

Like Thurber, we all face times when other people have doubts about what we can do and are very certain about what we can't. Sometimes we even get that way ourselves.

At such times, we have to stop and take stock. We can pray. We can look at our accomplishments. And we can ignore the doubts of others and move ahead. Only by trying do we stand a chance of learning our true capabilities.

> "Establish the counsel of your own heart, for no one is more faithful to you than it is."
> [SIRACH 37:13]

ಆ Guide us, Holy Spirit, to consult our innermost selves and not be deterred by external roadblocks.

DEPRESSION IS OFTEN thought of as an older person's illness. Not so, says Dr. Ghislaine Godenne. Teenagers are often depressed although their symptoms may differ.

In an article, "The Masked Signs of Adolescent Depression," Dr. Godenne cites delinquency, defiance, running away, poor grades, drugs, drinking and sexual promiscuity as signs of depression in youth.

"Depression is always a reaction to loss," notes Dr. Godenne, citing such childhood problems as lost self-esteem, lost dependence on parents, a lost sense of identity.

As adults we can forget how fragile we were as youths. We can fail to remember how seemingly minor incidents can be overwhelming to adolescents.

Remember how it was for you. Try to make it a little easier for a teenager today.

> "I led them with cords of compassion, with the bands of love."   [HOSEA 11:4]

✦ Father, may we ease the burden of pain which others are carrying.

ᏋACH YEAR in the United States, 10,000 pedestrians and bicyclists are killed and 500,000 injured. Many accidents occur at dusk or at night because a pedestrian or a car couldn't be seen.

"Don't be invisible when you walk along a dark road at night," says Allan A. Bass, Traffic Safety Coordinator for New Jersey's Middlesex County, "... wear bright-colored clothing."

Mr. Bass has a message for motorists, too.

"Low beam headlights (never parking lights) should be used in poor light conditions," he says. "It helps you see and be seen! Parking lights are illegal and hazardous; oncoming drivers may think they are the headlights of a distant car and it raises uncertainties on distance and speed."

Fixing blame, whether the crisis is in traffic or at home, doesn't help. By then, the damage has been done. Use care ahead of time. There may be something you can do yourself to avoid a "head-on" collision today—on the highway or in personal relationships.

"You have granted me life and steadfast love; and your care has preserved my spirit."
[JOB 10:12]

ᘓ   Help me to give a little more thought today, Lord, to the results of my actions.

THE "BIG, BAD WOLF," the "wolf at the door," the "wolf in sheep's clothing"—the wolf has had a bad name.

But biologists such as Dr. L. David Mech, who has studied wolves for 18 years and is an expert on the animal's behavior, are changing that image.

The once-hated creature is coming to be regarded as ecologically important to its wilderness habitats. It is now known not only as friendly and sociable within its pack, but as no threat to humans.

Dr. Mech is employed by the United States Fish and Wildlife Service. He is studying the northern Minnesota wolf population.

"We have a ways to go," says the biologist, "in changing people's attitudes about these animals."

Not only wolves suffer from erroneous attitudes. Just about any group of humans you can name has been discriminated against. It's time to put a stop to such treatment. You can help.

> "I will remember My covenant which is between Me and you and every living creature."
> [GENESIS 9:15]

Father, help us to view creation through Your eyes.

WHAT CONSTITUTES unethical conduct?

Businessmen aged 30-50 with salaries from $11,000 to $25,000 gave these answers during an executive development program:

1. Blaming errors on an innocent co-worker; 2. divulging confidential information; 3. falsifying reports; 4. taking credit for another's work; 5. padding expense accounts; 6. stealing company materials; 7. accepting gifts in exchange for better treatment; 8. giving such gifts/favors; 9. authorizing violation of rules; 10. calling in sick for day off; 11. hiding one's errors; 12. wasting time; 13. using company services for own gain; 14. doing own business on company time; 15. taking extra personal time; 16. not reporting rule violations.

Knowing what's wrong is a positive thing. Avoiding it is a lot better. Don't settle for being one of those people who "talk a good ballgame." Get in there and play—by the rules.

"The integrity of the upright guides them."
[PROVERBS 11:3]

๏ Holy Spirit, keep us honest on the job, and everywhere else.

 HOUSE CALL TO COLLECT for a cancer-fund drive saved the life of teenager Wade Scott.

When Mrs. R.A. Buce of Jonesboro, Georgia, was collecting for the Cancer Society, she asked one housewife, Mrs. J.E. Scott, if she knew the seven warning signs for cancer. After reading them to her, she left a brochure.

Two days later, Mrs. Scott noticed a large mole on her son Wade's foot. Remembering one of the danger signals, "an obvious change in a wart or mole," she took Wade to a doctor.

"He knew it was cancer before he operated," she recounted. "It was a malignant melanoma which is very dangerous. One day could mean the difference between life or death."

A thankful Mrs. Scott called the Cancer Society to find out who the volunteer was, and to offer her own services.

Take opportunities to step in when someone needs help. You can make a difference.

> "Wisdom abides in the mind of a man of understanding."   [PROVERBS 14:33]

❧   Grant us the wisdom, Father, to know when our action will help, and when it won't.

S⊤. LOUIS BARBER Bill Black not only relieves his customers of their hair—he also puts it back into the ecosystem as high-protein fertilizer.

Mr. Black collects the hair from his own shop and from other shops and beauty salons in the area. Working with handicapped persons and children in a garage equipped with a cement mixer, he sterilizes the hair, then mixes it with potting soil. The hair acts as a sponge, absorbing materials and releasing them through decomposition over a six-month period.

The end product, "B.J. Black's Ferthairlizer Potting Soil," won high praise from a spokesman for the Missouri Botanical Garden: "That man's idea is very good. It's a slow-release arrangement and a good food."

Mr. Black feels that his customers are pleased that "their hair is living on as someone else's plant."

Creativity—plant food from hair, reusable space shuttles, the Mona Lisa. God has made our minds mirrors of His. If we use them well, His will can be done "on earth as it is in heaven."

> "Be transformed by the renewal of your mind, that you may prove what is the will of God."
> [ROMANS 12:2]

Father, may we use our creativity in Your service.

CANOEING ALONE DOWN the Mississippi, Rebecca Johnson, 23, of Iowa City, Iowa, met plenty of people who said she'd never make it.

"When I got to within 200 miles of New Orleans, people asked me where I was going and then they'd say, 'Lady, that's a long way.' I'd say, 'Not when you've already paddled 2,200 miles,'" recalled Ms. Johnson. She started her 96-day trip in Minnesota, where the river begins.

"I've learned so much on this river. You learn about handling yourself. I think I could handle anything anybody wanted to throw at me now," the young woman said. Ms. Johnson recommends her trip to others. If you have "the stuff" then do it, she says.

Taking a chance can show us strengths we never knew we had. No one expects us to be foolhardy. But "playing it safe" is a sure way to reduce our chances of accomplishing anything. Do you dare to dare?

"Be strong, and of good courage. Fear not; be not dismayed." [1 CHRONICLES 22:13]

℮ Father, may our faith in You give us more courage.

FLORENCE EISEMAN OF MILWAUKEE, Wisconsin, turned a doctor's order into a family business.

"I was very nervous," Mrs. Eiseman recounts. Her doctor asked "Why don't you find something to do with your hands?" "I started sewing, and found I loved it." She made children's clothes.

Then the family had financial troubles, and Mrs. Eiseman sewed for customers. Her husband took samples of her work to Marshall Field in Chicago.

"He telephoned from Chicago and said he had sold Marshall Field an order for $30,000, and we didn't own one yard of material. And that was the start of the business."

The Eiseman sons, Robert and Laurence, joined the business. Says their mother, "I think it was rather glamorous for them to see an idea bloom as it did."

What do you "love" to do? Give it a try. You may discover that it's just what somebody else needs.

As we activate our potential, we begin to come alive in many ways.

"Do not neglect the gift you have."

[1 TIMOTHY 4:14]

ୡ   Give us the needed boost, Lord, to get out of our ruts and into something constructive.

THE BLACKFLY—cause of a disease known as river blindness—has struck 70,000 inhabitants in West African countries in the Volta River Basin.

The tide is turning. The World Health Organization, with the help of other United Nations agencies, the World Bank and a number of countries, has been combating the problem with a two-pronged campaign.

Black fly larvae are being sprayed with an otherwise harmless insecticide. A research program is developing treatment drugs. They're succeeding.

In villages classed in 1966 as highly affected, the proportion of victims fell from 50 percent to less than 10 percent. The disease in children rated 0.9 percent positive for those under 13 years old, as against 24 percent in those above 14, who were born before the campaign.

Health, nutrition, a decent place to live. Freedom of religion, free speech, government by choice rather than coercion. These rights can be achieved for all—with effort. Your effort.

> "Learn to do good; seek justice, correct oppression."
>
> [ISAIAH 1:17]

℮ Father, remind me that it's my world as much as anybody else's.

An ITEM FROM *The New York Times* may cheer those who wonder why "newspapers never print the good news."

Americo Pasquale of Hartford, Connecticut, runs a market that he took over when his father died. He had a surprise recently.

It seems that, in 1943, his father Jack had a customer named Michael Galovich who lost his credit at the market because of unpaid bills amounting to $173. Americo Pasquale just received a $185 money order marked "old bill." It was signed by Josephine Galovich, widow of the defaulter. After her husband's death, Mrs. Galovich discovered the original unpaid bills. She included the extra $12 to cover interest on the 35-year-old debt.

Said the amazed Mr. Pasquale, "It goes to show there are still some honest people in the world."

Most of us want to live in an "honest world." How about exercising some leadership? If someone suggested having the club newsletter run off on the machine at your office, would you point out that it would be wrong?

> "Have a clear conscience, desiring to act honorably in all things." [HEBREWS 13:18]

  Help us to remember, Lord, that we ourselves make our world what it is.

BOSTON SUBWAY RIDERS got more than a train ride for their money last summer—they were entertained.

"Music Under Boston" concerts—an experimental program of the Massachusetts Bay Transportation Authority—ranged from country and western to chamber music, from ragtime to rock. Most of the acts were local street musicians, such as Scrub Board Slim who performed before 20,000 commuters, while across town the Dixie Cook Book Band drew a similar audience.

According to Jeanne Lupin of the MBTA, the response was fantastic. "I've had people ask for schedules to find out who would be playing where and when."

One local resident said it was something to see the expression on people's faces after a hard day's work: "You should see the smiles."

A smile. So small, and yet a smile can do so much for everyone who is on the receiving end of one. As someone put it: "Be kind to everyone you meet. They may be having a tough day."

> "Our mouth was filled with laughter, and our tongue with shouts of joy."   [PSALM 126:2]

   Lord, make me quicker to smile, slower to frown.

T HERE'S AN UNUSUAL SIGHT on New York's Lower East Side—a windmill on a roof.

The three-blade turbine drives a 2,000-watt generator which produces enough electricity to light the building's hallways and pump hot water. The system provides 85 percent of the hot water used by the building's 11 tenants. A solar collector on the roof heats the water.

Tenants own the five-story building, a model for the area. Using Federal aid, they are rehabilitating it with another basic source of energy—human labor. A neighborhood project, Adopt-a-Building, calls it "sweat energy," payment for cooperative ownership.

The project may help solve the city's housing dilemma, says a city official, by providing "affordable housing" to low-income residents.

Human beings are often at their most creative when their "backs are against the wall." Intuition and thinking are elements of creativity, but there has to be hope. Can you give someone hope today?

> "'There is hope for your future,' says the Lord." [JEREMIAH 31:17]

 è May we make the small effort, Father, which may mean everything to another person.

FORESIGHT CAN PREVENT tragedies from fires, according to experts in the field.

Night fires are often fatal as sleeping families are overcome by smoke and gases. Hence, an effective smoke detector alarm system is a worthwhile investment. But a plan of escape is also needed. Follow these tips:

1. Draw a floor plan of your house; have at least two escape exits from bedrooms, allowing for blocking of stairs or halls by fire.

2. Have a warning system—if only a whistle.

3. Practice escaping.

4. Agree on a meeting place outdoors for a head count.

5. Sleep with bedroom doors closed.

6. Call the fire department from a neighbor's phone.

Some tragedies can't be prevented. But a few precautions can eliminate many and reduce the harm of others. If charity begins at home, one place to start would be to make fire safety a watchword in your house.

Alert others, too.

"Act accordingly, that you may be kept in safety."   [SIRACH 3:1]

ê Holy Spirit, remind us to keep our homes safe.

WHEN MENTALLY RETARDED handyman Herbert Woods died, citizens of St. Regis Falls, New York, provided a funeral befitting a loved and respected citizen.

Mr. Woods, a resident for seven years in a St. Regis Falls family care home, was a cheerful man who did odd jobs and helped around St. Ann's church and rectory. When he died at age 46, townspeople decided that his body should not be returned to the state institution which had placed him in family care.

The pastor donated a cemetery plot, the town's funeral director and interested families planned and conducted a wake and prayer service. Many sent flowers.

"Herbie was everybody's friend," said his family care provider. "He'd lived here, and we thought he belonged here with his friends in death, too."

It may be easier in a small community to show care for friends and neighbors than it is in a big city. But anywhere, one person can make a difference. Someone could use what you have to give. Who?

"May you be blessed by the Lord; for you have had compassion on me." [1 SAMUEL 23:21]

ℯ̂ Sharpen our vision, Holy Spirit, so we may see more clearly the secret hurts of others.

A CONVICTION THAT PEOPLE have a right to privacy was the foundation for Dan Patrick's firm, the Counter Measure Security Systems.

Mr. Patrick, 28, employs six electronics experts to find and remove electronic eavesdropping bugs from industrial and political offices.

He became interested in antibugging work after reading *The Electronic Invasion*, a book about the spread of eavesdropping devices. Noting the growing number of ads for surveillance equipment, he decided to fight bugging with a fulltime business.

"When you feel your privacy is in danger," he says, "it affects your life. It's a dirty business, and we would like to see a time when we would not be needed!"

Thanks to modern advances, there are many things we can do today that conscience may tell us we ought not. That is the test of our moral fiber.

Self-restraint for reasons of integrity is a sign that God is active in our lives.

"Keep your conscience clear." [1 PETER 3:16]

Give us the strength, Holy Spirit, to say "no" to actions that are profitable but questionable.

A 7-YEAR-OLD BOY's eight-mile run in darkness saved his 15-year-old uncle from quicksand in Wetumpka, Alabama.

Stumbling through rain-soaked woods, young Jeremy Mills and his puppy groped their way home from the spot where his uncle, Mark Payne, was sinking in quicksand. Before leaving Mark, Jeremy tied a rope to a tree for the older boy to hold onto.

Losing his way repeatedly, Jeremy followed his pup's barking, finally reaching home muddy and wet. Then, with his grandfather, Jeremy retraced the eight miles while rescue helicopters searched overhead.

"I was scared just a little," said the tired youngster after Mark was freed.

Perhaps, children can be helped toward maturity if parents put more trust in them.

Trust is one proof of love. It won't always succeed. But lack of trust never does. Children need love shown to them in practical ways. Developing the ability to let them go is a good place to start.

"I have great confidence in you."
[2 CORINTHIANS 7:4]

ჶ Give us a greater sense of confidence in all people, Lord, especially the young.

WHAT'S IN A NAME?

RISTOTLE TOTTLE WAS a pirate in Falmouth, England. So reports John Train in "Remarkable Names of Real People." And a chorister in the class of 1947 at Princeton was named Justin Tune.

Lawless & Lynch are attorneys in Jamaica, New York; and Ronald Supena, a lawyer in Philadelphia. And what of Dr. Zoltan Ovary, a New York gynecologist? I.C. Shivers is an iceman.

Would it have been better for Major Minor of the U.S. Army if he had joined the Navy instead? Or for Mrs. Screech to have been other than a singing teacher?

Could you have handled a name like Miss Horsey de Horsey, or Baroness Gaby von Bagge of Boo? A. Przybysz of Detroit, Michigan, changed his. To C. Przybysz.

A name can be awkwardly unique or, as a Smith or Jones may tell you, threaten one with anonymity. But in the long run, Shakespeare was probably right. "What's in a name?" Only the effort and concern we invest to be remembered as decent human beings who tried to make a difference during our short stay on earth.

"The days of a good life are numbered, but a good name endures for ever." [SIRACH 41:13]

Lord, may we judge people by who they are, not what they're called.

DISILLUSIONMENT, BOREDOM and failure now plague many of the young rebels of the 1960's, according to psychiatrists.

"People spent the 60's trying to get closer to each other," said New York's Dr. Leonard Bachelis, "But now they find something is missing."

Others said that some young persons appeared emotionally "burned out" after sampling drugs, many sexual partners and varied lifestyles.

Seattle psychologist Karol Marshall sees "a sense of helplessness, directionlessness and purposelessness. They seem to have been taught: 'You can expect to get what you want out of life.' Now they're finding that this philosophy doesn't necessarily work."

There is no "something for nothing." If there were, it probably wouldn't be worth it. To live a life takes lots of hard work, a sense of purpose and a little luck.

> "Before a man are life and death, and whichever he chooses will be given to him."
>
> [SIRACH 15:17]

ເຊ Strengthen our resolve, Father, to do something with our lives, especially when it seems hardest to do.

IN A YEAR'S TIME, Shimon Awerbuch and Steven Cohen have turned run-down blocks of near-slum property in Cohoes and Troy, New York, into 100 attractive homes.

Starting with the idea that much run-down housing is really a gem needing polishing, the two young men formed Tibbits Associates. They buy "tired" but sound housing, remodel it and rent it to moderate-income clients. Half are students.

"Everybody thinks students automatically mean disaster," says Mr. Awerbuch, "but we haven't had any problems. Give them good housing at good rates and they won't destroy it."

Now employing 10 persons full-time, the partners are marketing modern, renewed facilities for $13 to $15 per square foot, compared to the $20-per-square-foot cost of new construction.

Lots of us look at a problem and shrug. Shimon Awerbuch and Steven Cohen looked—and got going. They found a way to light a candle in one dark corner. How about you?

> "May the God of hope fill you with all joy and peace in believing, so that by the power of the Holy Spirit you may abound in hope."
> [ROMANS 15:13]

Jesus, You were guided by hope. Guide us in the same way.

A Northport, New York, jeweler was robbed of $200,000 worth of merchandise. He had no insurance. After his plight became known, the merchant saw a full-page ad in a local shopper's newspaper:

"Please Help a Fellow Friend and Businessman in Need," the headline read. The text mentioned the holdup and said that the owner might be forced out of business because of his loss. "Let us please help a fellow man," the ad went on. "For any future gifts, birthdays, anniversaries—even Christmas (it was August)—buy now and help a friend and local businessman get back on his feet."

Exacting a promise of anonymity, the advertiser agreed to an interview. Why did he do it? "I feel bad for him," he replied. And the anonymity? "I don't want him to feel obligated to me," said the man.

This modern version of the Good Samaritan story drives home the point Jesus made in telling the story. When He finished the parable He said, "Go, and do likewise." [LUKE 10:37]

eż Help me to be aware, Lord, of my neighbors' needs.

WHAT THE COUNTRY needs, says California cafe owner Jane Moss, is a good five-cent cup of coffee.

Mrs. Moss, who runs the Manor Burger in San Pablo, offered the nickel coffee to bring back customers after her shop was closed for two months. The gimmick worked so well she plans to keep the nickel price.

"It's my only advertising," said Mrs. Moss. Coffee is free with meals.

"Business is very good. I really can't complain at all," says the delighted restaurant owner.

We all love a bargain in these days of soaring costs and shrinking dollars. When the bargain recalls some of the good points of former times, it's doubly welcome.

A five-cent cup of coffee is a good idea. It has been for a long time. So are other "old-fashioned" things like loyalty, strong family ties, a fair day's work for a fair day's pay.

We could all use a little more of these old-fashioned ideas.

> "The fruit of the Spirit is love, joy, peace, patience, kindness, goodness, faithfulness, gentleness, self-control." [GALATIANS 5:22]

ếć Holy Spirit, show us what to cherish from the past.

Teenager Rod Sessum recently completed a term as Virginia City, Nevada's, only prisoner. According to him, it changed his life.

Deep into drugs, Rod was sentenced after robbing a hitchhiker. Because the old jail was cold and uncomfortable, local residents took the boy to their hearts. He was invited into homes for meals, and was free to roam the courthouse and attend high school games.

When the story of Rod Sessum's unusual "sentence" reached the papers, mail flooded in from Europe, Asia, Canada and all of the United States. He was even offered a scholarship by Sierra Nevada College.

Free after nine months for good behavior, Rod now has a job, a car, a girl friend and plans for college.

"When I got here, all I had was a pair of blue jeans," he says. "Now I've got a town full of friends. I've learned my lesson by people being nice to me."

"Love conquers all." It's old—but true. Try it. You'll see.

> "Repay no one evil for evil, but take thought for what is noble in the sight of all."
> [ROMANS 12:17]

e² Father, may we be effective instruments of Your love.

Is THERE ROOM for emotion in medical care? Some experts think the answer is yes.

● "I can't get emotionally involved," doctors and nurses constantly tell University of California psychologist, Dr. Charles Garfield. He stresses the patient's need for emotional support.

● Sally Brooks of the University of California Nursing Service believes compassion may, for some, be more important than the physical care.

● Dr. Daniel Federman of Stanford University School of Medicine thinks the complexity of modern medicine interferes with the doctor-patient relationship. "The chance to express some of the personal feelings of caring," he says "is . . . limited by the urgency of the care."

Doctors and nurses do face special problems. But is there anything keeping you and me from spending time with one person who is lonely? Or, with one who is suffering, hungry, broken-hearted, or just afraid? It costs so little—and can do so much.

"Love is patient and kind."

[1 CORINTHIANS 13:4]

Help me, Lord, to be filled with the love You show us every day.

I N THE BUSY, NOISY world in which we live, silence is sometimes found embarrassing, often boring.

German theologian Bernard Haering had weeks of enforced silence when throat cancer struck him. He underwent a series of operations and received an artificial vocal chord. Later, he had this to say:

"Do you know that in America silence is for sale? The juke boxes have mute records, so that anyone who wants to rest his ears can put in a quarter and enjoy three minutes of silence.

"I had five weeks of silence for free, and it taught me that life is a continuous conversation."

The priest spoke of his thoughts at the prospect of being forever mute. "I thought that God was giving me the chance for a contemplative life ... During the five weeks of silence, I lived out my hope."

In silence, we can weigh our everyday experiences and make better choices. In silence, we can more deeply experience ourselves, and God.

> "Oh that you would keep silent, and it would be your wisdom." [JOB 13:5]

ᶜᶓ   Help us, Father, to seek the silence which will enable us to live more deeply.

T HE WORLD'S LARGEST LIBRARIES are hurrying to microfilm tens of millions of books before their pages fall apart. And they're losing.

"You can't comprehend a century's books disappearing, but that's what's happening," says a Columbia University restorer. The books, of 19th and 20th century vintage, crumble within 50 to 75 years, eaten by the acids with which the bookpaper was manufactured.

The use of alum resin in printing papers, begun in the United States in 1840, causes books literally to "burn up." Preservationists predict a huge printed record gap in 19th and 20th century publications due to an unwitting mistake by early paper manufacturers.

For us as individuals and as a society, acting without weighing the consequences is an unaffordable luxury. In all you do, look ahead. Plan. Weigh your words and actions.

The danger in leaping before you look is that, without expecting to, you just may land in hot water.

"The prudent looks where he is going."
[PROVERBS 14:15]

℮ Father, make us wise servants.

THERE'S SAFETY in numbers, says Allan A. Bass of the Middlesex County Traffic Safety Bureau. Mr. Bass is appalled by the fact that traffic crashes in this country kill five people every hour.

How can we get the safety message across? Allan Bass would give grandparents a chance at it. "There are almost 25 million Americans over 65," he says, maintaining that America's grandparents represent a largely untapped resource.

Mr. Bass sees grandparents as having a big stake in safety and suggests they get into community programs. They also have a pretty wide area of influence right in the family, he notes. "Children growing up in a 'world of wheels' must have constant reminders."

The big influence in a child's life is the way the adults in the family live, and there is truth in the slogan, "You Drive As You Live." Relaxed or frenzied, courteous or rude, careful or reckless. How about you—parents and grandparents?

> "You have observed my teaching, my conduct, my aim in life, my faith, my patience, my love." [2 TIMOTHY 3:10]

> Lord, may we realize the power of the example we set.

Ɲᴇᴡ Yᴏʀᴋ's Pᴀʟᴇʏ Pᴀʀᴋ has proved to city dwellers that "beauty" doesn't have to be "big." The minipark is a sanctuary for office workers, shoppers and tourists.

A gift to the city from CBS chairman William S. Paley, the pocket-size park occupies just 42 x 100 feet on Manhattan's 53rd Street between Fifth and Madison Avenues.

Tourists' first awareness of the park often comes as they hear the unlikely sound of running water, while strolling on 53rd Street. It comes from a sheet of water tumbling down the 20-foot high wall at the rear of the park. Graceful locust trees form a delicate canopy for visitors. Chairs and tables provide a place for a quiet lunch, or just a rest.

Beauty can be big or small. Either way, it takes inner vision, thoughtful planning and skillful execution. There can be beauty in our lives as well as our works. Beauty is one of God's gifts, bringing joy to life.

> "I will watch over them to build and to plant, says the Lord." [JEREMIAH 31:28]

ᥱᴈ Make our actions reflect the goodness and beauty, Lord, that is Yours.

HAVE YOU EVER DIALED a phone number and heard: "The number you have reached is not in service at this time," etc., etc.?

If so, chances are good that you've been listening to Jane Barbe, the recorded voice for telephone companies throughout the country. Each day this mother of two teenagers tells six to eight million dialers the time, temperature or that they have reached a wrong number. Mrs. Barbe, who does her messages for Audichron Company of Atlanta, has a drama degree from the University of Georgia and has worked as a singer. Since she talks to people used to hearing regional accents she has to be careful and can, in fact, adjust her voice for her audience.

Most of us don't speak to millions. But we do have a share of God's truth to communicate to those who cross our path. Think, consider your hearer, take the long view. Communicate as you would be communicated with. It's a sure-fire formula—no matter how large, or small, your audience is. And it's always the right number.

"Consider it, take counsel, and speak."
[JUDGES 19:30]

   Lord, make us instruments of Your truth.

AMERICANS CAME TO KNOW of William Shakespeare and his writings through the "rowdies" of the Western frontier, not the sophisticated Easterners, claims author Alistair Cooke.

"There is no need at all to wonder what the founders of New England thought about Shakespeare," he says. "They didn't. In all the colonial literature of the 17th century there is not, I believe, a single allusion to him."

Mr. Cooke points out that knowledge of the bard "came from strolling players who followed flatboats...and rode into rowdier pioneer towns..." The rough and tumble of Shakespeare matched the frontier's appetite for rowdiness, according to the critic and commentator. These tough audiences, not Easterners, made us aware of Shakespeare.

Romeo and Juliet in a rough frontier settlement—life is full of surprises. That's why it's so important to keep both our eyes and our minds open. We never know where God is speaking to us—or through whom.

> "If you love to listen you will gain knowledge, and if you incline your ear you will become wise."   [SIRACH 6:33]

Father, may we listen for Your voice and learn to expect it in unlikely places.

To THOUSANDS OF AUSTRALIANS, the family doctor is a computer.

As part of the free government medical program, patients talk with the computers by pressing buttons to answer questions appearing on a TV-like screen.

Following 40 minutes of button pushing, the patient goes with a nurse for X-rays, blood tests and other examinations. The full battery of questions and tests lasts between 90 and 105 minutes.

Called Medicheck, the program was started by a $1-million foundation set up by philanthropist Sir William Tyree. In two years, its popularity grew until it now takes two months to "get an appointment with the computer."

Putting technology to work to spread the benefits of modern medicine is a good idea.

While no machine can replace the health worker who cares about people, it can supplement such efforts. That leaves persons free to do what they do best—care.

"Whatever you do, do all to the glory of God."
[1 CORINTHIANS 10:31]

Widen our vision, Holy Spirit, to what good results may be obtained from technical advances.

FOR PRIMITIVE people, healing and religious belief were intertwined. Are we so different?

Margaret Schlientz, former chairman of Marquette University's psychiatric nursing department, has found that the patients she prayed with made tremendous progress.

She believes that collaboration between psychiatrists and spiritual directors has great possibilities. "You don't rely on psychiatry alone," she says, "you don't rely on prayer alone. The two go together."

Miss Schlientz herself embodies that combination. Still a member of the nursing faculty, she is also a candidate for a master of Christian spirituality degree at Creighton University.

"Prayer," she says, "can teach people to open themselves up to God, and then the healing can begin."

There isn't one of us who doesn't need healing of one kind or another. Prayer is a prescription any of us can try.

"He grants healing, life and blessing."
[SIRACH 34:17]

eȝ   Lord, help us to turn to You in faith.

Do YOU HAVE TROUBLE asserting yourself? The *San Francisco Examiner* offers tips:

1. Make eye contact. People have to reckon with you when you look them straight in the eye.

2. Speak up. A strong confident voice tells people you're not a pushover.

3. Be decisive in your words and actions. Fully completed gestures and sentences indicate you are sure of yourself and of getting what you want.

4. Stand tall and you'll act tall.

5. When something bothers you, don't clam up. Address yourself to someone who can correct it.

6. Talk in an expressive fashion. A monotone turns people off.

7. Learn to nod. It provides instant feedback to others.

8. Develop a firm handshake, one that says you're not afraid of contact with others.

Only when others are aware of your presence, can you make a difference in the world.

"You are the light of the world."

[MATTHEW 5:14]

ε̃ In my personal growth, Father, may I remember that you have a job for me to do.

A NORWEGIAN FATHER TOLD his 9-year-old son about the world's very poor children. The boy thought it over.

Then the boy—his name is Jaran Dammann—and his friends decided to start a magazine to tell children about youngsters in poor countries. "If all the children in Norway stopped drinking Coca Cola," wrote Jaran in one issue, "just think how much money we could send to the poor children."

The young publishers manage to make about $25 on each monthly issue. They send the money directly to a children's hospital in Kaziba, Africa.

"To Jaran it's very simple," says his father. "'If we have too much, why don't we give it to those who have too little?' he asks. He can't understand why adults don't look at it this way."

Unfortunately, it isn't quite as simple as it seems to Jaran. But if we were to take more seriously such simplicity, some important things might begin to happen. None of us has to look very far for the poor.

"Blessed is he who considers the poor."

[PSALM 41:1]

eð Father, may we follow Your Son in loving and in giving.

THE JASPERS SAW this ad in the newspaper: "Families needed to board outpatients from a mental-health center." After some hesitation, they answered it.

Edith Jasper and her middle-aged daughter, Gloria, of Bergen County, New Jersey, have made Jane, who is in her sixties, a part of the family. She no longer needs to be in the psychiatric hospital where she had spent a number of years. But she does need a family.

The Dumont Center for Community Mental Health pays the Jaspers $200 a month for board and room.

In another case, a lonely middle-aged bachelor took in a man about his own age. The foster family program benefits everybody. Says psychiatric social worker Stephanie Miller, "It's nice for both groups to have a family."

Some of the most successful solutions to human problems are those that put together, like jigsaw pieces, people who need each other. Try it in your own life. You may be able to unscramble a puzzle.

"Increase and abound in love to one another and to all men." [1 THESSALONIANS 3:12]

ও   May I use my ingenuity and love, Lord, to make life more livable for someone else.

A NEW CREDIT UNION opened in Oregon with its membership limited solely to felons and ex-felons.

"By creating a financial institution designed especially to take care of emergency needs, we will be helping ex-felons cope with crisis and remain lawful members of society," said state corrections administrator Bob Watson.

The idea for a credit union to hold the savings and make loans just for prison inmates and former inmates was partly due to the problems such persons have in getting loans from regular banks.

"We have found the inability to establish credit and maintain financial stability during the first critical months after release from prison increases the individual's chance of failure," says Mr. Watson.

It's easy to forget the difficulties faced by those who are trying to reenter society after paying their debt to it. Easy, but very costly in the long run.

Give an occasional thought and prayer to ex-convicts. It just may lead to action.

Remember, Jesus said: "I was in prison and you came to Me." [MATTHEW 25:36]

  Remind me that a prison is made of people, Lord.

h **ALF OF THOSE RESPONDING** to a national survey of the Epilepsy Foundation of America said that their disease had kept them from jobs.

One woman who had used part-time work to finance her undergraduate and graduate education wrote:

"...I hoped for the day when I would be able to apply this education. I find...that employers are still reluctant to accept the handicapped...

"When one applies for a position, he no longer has to admit to his intention to work against our government, yet I must admit to a physical handicap which in no way would hinder the performance I could render.

"It is ironic that I am not seriously enough handicapped to qualify for...Social Security benefits, yet I cannot do what I want to do most—WORK..."

All of us know what it's like to want just a chance to show someone what we really are, what we can do. To give another person that chance is to "love your neighbor as yourself," as Jesus taught.

> "By this all men will know that you are My disciples, if you have love for one another."
> [JOHN 13:35]

ð We say we are Your followers, Jesus. Remind us to check the path we are on to be sure it is Yours.

MITCHELL KORN'S JOB is looking for "lost people." Mr. Korn, 29, directs New York City's Murray Hill SRO (Single Room Occupancy) Project.

Teams of workers search for the old and withdrawn in 29 hotels and rooming houses.

"These are the people who are not touched by anyone else," Mr. Korn points out. "The people in SRO's are at the total end of the road. For some, it is the first time in 10 years they have let someone into their rooms."

Medical care, food and clothing are provided by SRO, then individual rehabilitation. Explains Mr. Korn, "If they need it, we give it. We're trying to create a total environment of dignity and support."

Tragedy, fear, heartache—they have hit people near you. They may not be at the "end of the road." But they are isolated—and hurting.

Pick up a phone, ring a doorbell, write a note. You may comfort one of God's suffering children.

> "Comfort those who are in any affliction, with the comfort with which we ourselves are comforted by God." [2 CORINTHIANS 1:4]

℮ Holy Spirit, show us where—and how—to help the hurting.

AN OCTOGENARIAN COUPLE in Burlington, Wisconsin, telephone over 1,000 people a year.

When Harry and Leona Terry dial a number, the person who picks up the phone at the other end hears: "Happy Birthday to You" sung in duet.

The Terry's always called their 14 grandchildren on their birthdays. "Then one day we called a friend up, singing 'Happy Birthday,'" says Mrs. Terry, "and she was so appreciative she had us call a friend of hers." That was the start.

Now those who request it, no matter how far away, receive a yearly greeting at just the cost of the call.

"The folks are always so happy with this little personal touch in their lives," says Harry Terry, "that it makes us happy, too." His wife adds, "We always have a nice little visit with folks we call."

How many of us picture ourselves in our 80's deeply involved and useful in serving others? We can. Loving is simple.

"Love never ends."   [1 CORINTHIANS 13:8]

ॐ   Help me, Lord, to understand that as long as I
       live, my love will be needed.

Almost 3,000 youngsters in King County, Washington, may avoid the Juvenile Court system and Youth Center each year thanks to "neighborhood courts."

Composed of volunteers who donate their time, the courts meet with parents and children in misdemeanor cases: truancy, tampering with fire alarms, shoplifting and first-time drug use. Although volunteers have no power to enforce their decisions, most families follow their recommendations to avoid court intervention.

"When we have the confidence of the child and the parents," says one volunteer, "then we go to work on the problem. That's when we're accomplishing something."

If you want people's confidence, ask yourself: Am I prepared to earn the trust of others by showing an unflagging concern for the things that matter to them? Will I pitch in when help is needed? Will I "hang in" when things get tough?

> "For the measure you give will be the measure you get back." [LUKE 6:38]

ぞ Help us, Father, to persevere in loving our neighbor.

Michael Larsen, a San Francisco literary agent, reminds writers of their power to stimulate awareness, propose solutions and inspire change.

Mr. Larsen uses the *Whole Earth Catalog*, a best-seller in the late 1960's, as an example of a book that gave to a generation of Americans a vision:

"A lifestyle replacing the artificial with the natural, consumption with simplicity, possessions with experience, economic growth with personal growth, the desire for more with the need for enough."

Then he throws down the gauntlet to writers to:

"Help us to realize our gifts and motivate us to use them...

"Provide us with works of art that uplift our spirits and make us believe in ourselves."

A gift for writing—or for painting, organizing, listening, whatever it may be—carries with it a responsibility and a challenge. While it has the stamp of uniqueness, God gave it to each of us to use in His service, to make a better world.

"Having gifts that differ... let us use them."
[ROMANS 12:6]

May I accept my gifts, Lord, with gratitude and use them to serve You.

Tiny plants grown in test tubes in Marion Mapes's laboratory may someday feed a hungry world.

Mrs. Mapes, a noted plant physiologist, hopes that her University of Hawaii laboratory will find the key to developing super plants that are disease resistant and can survive heavy or sparse rainfall. If she succeeds, productive superior plants could be reproduced exactly and sent to poor countries.

Mrs. Mapes takes cells from adult plant tissue and treats them in the test tube with growth-stimulating chemicals, causing identical plants to grow.

"What we want is a plant exactly like the mother plant," she explains. Then "we can produce great numbers of food-bearing plants in test tubes. These plants can be transported for planting in other parts of the world."

The war on hunger is being waged on many fronts: laboratories, government offices, classrooms, experimental farms. Are you working and praying for the day when all will have enough to eat?

"I was hungry and you gave Me food."

[MATTHEW 25:35]

Lord, help us to find effective ways to feed the hungry.

SYLVIA LAUDON OF FAIRFIELD, Iowa, retired recently from her job as a secretary. She is 67. Retired?

Mrs. Laudon writes weekly to her six sisters. She keeps up, too, with her 21 nieces and nephews and 24 grandnieces and grandnephews, at least on special days.

She cares for her disabled husband Elmer. Then there are two daughters, a son, and seven grandchildren. She keeps in touch by phone or citizen's band radio. She also grows and cans vegetables.

Recently a niece found in her mailbox a letter from Mrs. Laudon about snapdragons, family news, putting up catsup, and a touch of philosophy.

"Reading this," she told a friend, "I couldn't help but feel all's right with the world after all."

At 67, Sylvia Laudon may have a lot more "get up and go" than most people. Even if you can't keep her pace, ask yourself how much you are putting into your day. After all, we usually get back from life just about as much as we invest in it.

"Choose life, that you and your descendants may live." [DEUTERONOMY 30:19]

ɞ Lord, give us joy in living.

EARNING AN EMPLOYEE's confidence doesn't just happen. The Organizational Behavior Institute gives these pointers for building trust:

● Don't overstate your case, exaggerate or make promises you can't keep.

● Don't be humorless about yourself, but *never* use humor in correcting a subordinate.

● Don't box yourself in. Being unable to retreat gracefully erodes confidence.

● Don't discourage criticism. The kibitzer can keep you from playing the wrong card.

● Don't ignore your own limitations. True self-confidence depends on knowing your weaknesses.

● Don't be a "bargainer." Avoid stratagems and tactics. Outmaneuvering an individual will only make him wary.

The surest way to gain another's confidence is to show by our consistent interest and attention that we are genuinely interested in him or her. It's a very practical way of loving our neighbor as ourselves.

"Aim at righteousness, faith, love, and peace."
[2 TIMOTHY 2:22]

℞ Holy Spirit, keep us open with love toward each other.

Dorothy N. Garrett read a book about ministry to the dying in India, and things began to happen in Virginia.

Inspired by Malcolm Muggeridge's *Mother Teresa: Something Beautiful for God*, Ms. Garrett decided "there should be a community service to do something beautiful for the living." Hence, HAVEN of Northern Virginia.

In six months, 60 people had volunteered. They are trained in the art of listening, interviewing and counseling persons faced with life-threatening illness.

Workers help in the hospital and at home, at bedside and by phone, with secondary nursing care and just caring.

"Every time I mentioned the idea to someone," says Ms. Garrett, "the response was 'What can I do to help?'"

One person becomes 60 people. Many of us want to help. But, we need the problem made visible. We need a leader. If you want, you can be one.

"Rejoice with those who rejoice. Weep with those who weep." [ROMANS 12:15]

Help me, Holy Spirit, to go beyond myself—to be more concerned with human need.

READERS OF TWO SOUTHERN NEWSPAPERS may have been startled recently to see an ad for a doctor—in the sports section.

The ad appeared in the *Nashville Tennessean* and the *Lexington Herald.* "Doctor needed in city of Greenville, Kentucky," it ran. "Salary $57,000. No prior experience needed. Malpractice paid. Hard up. Contact Willard Keith."

One critic said it was demeaning to the profession. Willard Keith, of Muhlenberg County Hospital, admits his unorthodoxy. But Greenville got its doctor.

"I wanted it to be read, of course, and people read the sports section ... We got five or six calls right away. Why not advertise? Why not say what you mean?"

Concern for the structure of a profession, a business, a university can eclipse the needs of people those institutions were designed to serve. With caring and some creative thinking, you can reach your target.

> "The sabbath was made for man, not man for the sabbath." [MARK 2:27]

ễ   Help me, Lord, to have the vision to see what is important in each situation.

ᴮECAUSE OF ONE NEW YORK police officer, 150,000 youngsters a year are involved in a city-wide basketball program.

Dennis Fitzgerald started by organizing police basketball teams for the neighborhood kids to watch. Then he organized contests for the youngsters themselves.

The games grew in popularity. Private businesses donated funds for team T-shirts. Basketballs were bought to be given as prizes. Now a city-wide program, the police-sponsored games attract thousands of urban teenagers. Some are held at intermission time in Madison Square Garden during pro games.

What can one person do? All kinds of things. Dennis Fitzgerald started where he was, on his job. If you have a job, you might start lighting candles there. If not, you have a neighborhood, a family. The opportunity to serve is as close as the person next to you.

"If anyone serves Me, he must follow Me."
[JOHN 12:26]

Father, may we look for ways to serve.

ONE OF THE WEST'S FASTEST horsemen is a 28-year-old rancher with one arm, no legs and only one eye.

Jim Brunotte, who lost his legs, arm and an eye near Long Binh, Vietnam, in 1968, runs a 367-acre ranch at Creston, California. In United States and Canadian horse shows, he has won over 200 trophies in speed riding and other contests against non-handicapped men.

Mr. Brunotte runs Rancho Kumbya, a non-profit ranch where handicapped persons learn swimming, riding, skiing and skeet shooting. Most memorable of all, they see Mr. Brunotte caring for livestock, saddling horses and swinging from his wheelchair onto his horse's back. "People like me have to hang in there," he says. "I have a lot to live for."

Once again, we see that "handicapped" as a label is probably more disabling than the physical disability that gives rise to the term.

Don't label the handicapped. Enable. Enable them to give all they've got. And that's a lot.

> "Decide never to put a stumbling block or hindrance in the way of a brother."
>
> [ROMANS 14:13]

Jesus, You saw the person, not the handicap. May we do the same.

IN ONE CALIFORNIA COUNTY, 11,000 long-toed salamanders have everything their way.

To make sure that the fast-vanishing Santa Cruz salamander can wander freely in seeking food and shelter, the county board of supervisors voted unanimously to adopt new building regulations in a square mile of land around the pond and lagoon where the little orange reptiles live:

Curbs must be rounded. Houses on slopes must have crawl space underneath. Grading must be minimal to protect underbrush. And retaining walls 100 feet long must have special "salamander ramps" for crossing.

Supervisor Dale Dawson, whose county district has the two last habitats of the little creatures, says the long-toes have been around for 50,000 years, and deserve a right to coexist with humans.

How do we look at the world? As a domain in which nature must be subdued to the human will? Or as God's good earth, in which there is ample room for all His creatures?

"All these things My hand has made, and so all these things are mine, says the Lord."
[ISAIAH 66:2]

Change our perspective, Creator of all, so that we see Your world as a whole.

LVIN PEYTON CAN'T SEE. But for 15 years he has repaired the machines at his three self-service laundries.

"When I bought the first laundromat, I got a repair manual," says Mr. Peyton, a man in his sixties. His wife Irene read the manual to him, and he learned to repair by feel. "I had an advantage. Washing machines are close to the floor and you can't see in there unless you lie on your stomach. I can just sit in front and reach in there," he says.

"It's a pleasure to watch him work," says a friend, Buzz Anderson. Not that Mr. Peyton is "all work". He enjoys playing poker with Braille cards.

Some people meet setbacks and spend the rest of their lives lamenting what they can't do. Others, like Alvin Peyton, go very far with what they've got. Which approach do you think "lights candles"? "It is better to light one candle than to curse the darkness."

> "Let him labor...so that he may be able to give to those in need."   [EPHESIANS 4:28]

℮ℓ   Lord, may we emphasize the positive in our lives.

EMPLOYEES IN A PAPER BAG FACTORY are getting the chance to sign their handiwork.

When the St. Regis Paper Company's plant in Vernon, California, had a quality-control problem, employees were asked how to cut the reject rate. They suggested that making each worker responsible for his or her production would do the trick.

Each bag now bears the maker's initials. Productivity is higher and employee morale is up.

The plant's rejection rate is less than half of one percent, and workers agree personal pride made the difference.

To want people to know we've passed this way is a common—and legitimate—human longing. Whether it's an initialed paper bag or ages-old graffiti found in ancient excavations, as long as humans could make their mark they have left evidence of their passing.

You're unique. Cherish what is special in you. Use it to leave a lasting mark on the world around you—by leaving it better because you passed through.

> "Whatever your task, work heartily, as serving the Lord and not men." [COLOSSIANS 3:23]

Holy Spirit, show us ways to make a lasting, positive difference.

Two THIRDS OF OUR CHILDREN live in unnecessary fear, says a national survey of youngsters aged 7 to 11. The survey's findings were released by the Foundation for Child Development.

- A fourth of the children queried are afraid of the programs they watch on TV.
- Two thirds fear someone "bad" may enter their homes.
- Half said they could watch TV whenever they want.
- A third said they wished they had more of their mother's time, while half said they wanted to see their fathers more. A fourth did not even have their fathers living with them.

When parents are not there, or are not open in showing love, fear moves into the vacuum.

We all need love. We can't "make" another love us, but we can try to give love unselfishly.

Love is the gift of God. It comes freely from the Source, and it can grow as we give it away.

"Perfect love casts out fear." [1 JOHN 4:18]

ख़ Increase our generosity, Jesus, so we may learn to live as You lived.

THE COMPUTER AGE intimidates many of us. But it has its good side.

Enter the microcomputer—into our homes. They are built into sewing machines, stoves, and other appliances to eliminate hundreds of parts and increase usefulness.

Home computers with keyboards and videomonitors can control the lights, heat and air-conditioning to increase efficiency and decrease fuel bills; alert you to water seepage in the basement. They can tutor your children in math or languages, help balance your checkbook and figure your income tax, and, if you're self-employed, handle the bookkeeping.

One man has programmed a computer, attached to a sensing device under his baby's mattress, to monitor heartbeat and respiration. Any irregularity would set off an alarm—a protection against "crib death."

God created us with reason and imagination. As free human beings we can choose to use them in His service. Rather than resist technology, we would better serve by using its tools to make a better world.

"Have the mind of Christ."

[1 CORINTHIANS 2:16]

Help us, Lord, in our modern world, to match our expertise with integrity and good will.

IF YOU LIVED in Austin, Nevada, Kittie Bonner could cut your hair, bake you a cake or haul you into jail for breaking the law.

Kittie Bonner, 75, was appointed constable of the once-booming silver-mining town 13 years ago, shortly after the death of her husband, who was deputy sheriff. She carries a gun but has never used it. Although she has led armed posses, most of her work is in the Lander County Courthouse where she serves as bailiff.

At other times, she serves on the Red Cross board as she has for 42 years, or dusts off the old barber chair in her living room for an occasional customer.

She has baked cakes for many an Austin wedding.

People need to feel they are really part of something—a business enterprise, a community, a parish, the family. Think of ways to use the ability of people—young and old—so that they will feel needed—because the need is real.

> "Now there are varieties of gifts, but the same spirit." [1 CORINTHIANS 12:4]

&ebdot; Give me the ingenuity and the courage, Lord, to make myself useful to others, whatever my age.

Twenty years ago, computer-systems designer Shane Dickey made tests which convinced him that using the sun to heat or cool homes was technically possible. In 1975, he began building his solar dream house.

But so far he hasn't been able to finish it due to financial and zoning obstacles. The necessary 35-foot-high roof exceeded county limits, so Mr. Dickey applied for a variance. The bank wouldn't lend money for the solar heating system, so he got a loan for his backup electrical system. Mr. Dickey also had trouble finding an architect enthusiastic about his housing ideas.

One researcher in solar energy says that just about everything needed for solar heating is being manufactured. Cooperation, he claims, is the big factor. "All we need to do," he adds "is pull it together."

Cold winters and high fuel bills have made us more energy-conscious. But our ways of thinking and acting need to be changed for us to be good "energy savers."

The question is: Are we willing to change?

> "You know how to interpret the appearance of the sky, but you cannot interpret the signs of the times." [MATTHEW 16:3]

ẽ͡ Help us to be alert to what is going on in the world, Lord, so we may be ready for the future.

For Irene Auberlin, it didn't require either youth or wealth to reach out to the entire world.

Mrs. Auberlin, now a widowed 80-year-old grandmother, has been the guiding force behind an organization which in 23 years has sent over $240 million in free medical and dental supplies to missionary hospitals all over the world.

Working in a drafty, eight-story warehouse in a Detroit ghetto, Mrs. Auberlin is president of World Medical Relief, Inc., a nonprofit, nondenominational organization dedicated to helping the world's sick poor.

WMR channels medicines, surgical equipment and funds from donors to hospitals and clinics in poor areas. Some hospitals have been equipped from the ground up.

How much poorer those hospitals would be if Irene Auberlin didn't start doing something a quarter of a century ago. And how much better off someone you know might be if you decide, with God's help, to do something constructive today.

"Rescue the weak and the needy."

[PSALM 82:3]

Give us a better sense of people's needs, Jesus, and help us do something to meet them.

IT WOULD BE GREAT if there were a way to save an additional 55,000 lives each year from cancer.

There is. Prevention. According to the American Cancer Society, there are six specific sites where the disease could be reduced by prevention or early detection.

LUNGS - Don't smoke cigarettes; at least cut down.

SKIN - Protect it from too much sun with lotions, hats, beach umbrellas. Watch sores that don't heal.

MOUTH - Have your doctor or dentist check it.

COLON - If over 40, have a proctoscopic examination.

BREAST - Do monthly breast self-examination.

UTERUS - Pap test yearly for women over 20.

It's still true: "An ounce of prevention is worth a pound of cure." Where cancer is concerned, it's not only worth it, it is a matter of life and death. Take care of yourself. You're all you've got.

"Before you fall ill, take care of your health."
[SIRACH 18:19]

ඥ Father, make us health-minded with regard to ourselves and others.

HMOUNTAIN OF DISCARDED food gave youngsters at Camarillo, California's Pleasant Valley School a dramatic lesson on waste.

After watching pupils dump food into garbage cans during lunch hour, principal Jerry Moynihan gathered the 450 students together, then emptied the contents of the nearest trash can onto a table.

The inventory: 41 wrapped sandwiches, 19 apples, 13 oranges, two cartons of milk, 19 candy bars, 14 cookies and dozens of other untouched foods. Then Mr. Moynihan sent a letter to parents itemizing what he found, and teachers began lessons on food waste.

"Since we did this," says Mr. Moynihan, "parents have been saying 'Wow, I didn't know this was happening.' The kids were impressed. Seeing it was the dramatic part of it."

The most effective way we learn is not through abstract propositions but through specific examples. Whether it's a lesson on waste, selfishness or any other subject, find a way to dramatize your point.

> "I have given you an example, that you also should do as I have done to you."
>
> [JOHN 13:15]

Help us, Father, to communicate important points by finding an apt example.

A CHILDHOOD LOVE of windmills led 55-year-old Nel-leken Muysken to make her home in a 350-year-old Dutch mill near Amsterdam.

With her husband Matthys, a nuclear engineer, Mrs. Muysken took over the mill in 1968. They spent nine months renovating the ancient structure into a comfortable three-story home. No longer used for pumping canal water, the mill still operates because "everyone in town likes to see the mill turning. It reminds them of the good old days."

Mrs. Muysken, as miller-in-residence, cares for her own mill and those around it being preserved as historical buildings. "I've been fascinated by windmills since childhood," she says. "It was fulfilling a dream to finally live in one."

In an age of rapid change, a windmill stands as a symbol of continuity.

Many things are in need of change—even cry out for it. But some things, like dependability, faithfulness and love, need to be preserved in any age.

> "Aim at righteousness, godliness, faith, love, steadfastness, gentleness." [1 TIMOTHY 6:11]

ᥱᨃ Give us the wisdom, Holy Spirit, to know how to make progress that protects the good things of life.

WHAT'S IN A NAME? A lot of problems if you live in Sweden and your name is Johansson.

One out of every 15 people in Sweden is named Johansson. There are 62 pages of Johanssons in the Stockholm telephone directory. The situation generates irritations and even dangers, with the same name, and even X-rays getting switched between patients.

To help solve the problem, the Swedish government has given all its citizens a "person number"—a 10-digit identification code. It also encourages all Johanssons to change their names for a fee of $8. In one year, 5,000 Swedes did so.

Even if bureaucracies mix us up, each of us is still unique. Each has strengths, talents, emotions and even shortcomings that no one else has in quite the same way.

To make the most of our powers and reduce our liabilities is a lifetime job. It requires insight, honesty, hard work and prayer. God wants our growth as persons and will help us.

> "I will give them an everlasting name which shall not be cut off." [ISAIAH 56:5]

Make me more aware of who I am, Lord, and more eager to become a better person.

COUNTING TO TEN when she was angry was an effective way to "cool off" for Grace Oursler, until she discovered a better way.

The late executive editor of *Guideposts* magazine always used the "count-to-ten" idea until she noticed that the opening phrase of the Lord's Prayer also had ten words. She tried repeating them instead of numbers. It worked much better. Then she found that when she was very angry, repeating the phrase ten times broke the power of her anger completely.

Sometimes anger is justified—for instance, indignation over cruel or careless behavior. But that doesn't include the right to call people bad names, put them down or injure them.

By saying, "I am upset because..." instead of "You..." we can often redirect anger into a constructive action.

And a quick prayer—like the Our Father—can help us put our feelings and another's actions into proper perspective.

"Our Father, Who art in heaven, hallowed be Thy Name." [MATTHEW 6:9]

ﻣ Help us to make strong feelings work for better communication, Father, instead of spoiling our relationships.

Tiny Carolyn Keber will probably live to grow up because Georgetown University doctors devised an alarm system to guard her against crib death.

The two-month-old baby daughter of the Vincent Kebers of Gaithersburg, Maryland, sleeps with an electronic monitor connected to her chest. It sounds a beeping alarm when her breathing stops for 30 seconds. It has already saved the baby's life eight times.

Carolyn has a rare, inherited disease that can lead to crib death, and a brother and four relatives of the Kebers have already died of the mysterious condition.

"Doctors must become much more aware," says Dr. Paul Sandler of Georgetown, "that these deaths do often run in families." Some parents, he said, are told, "'Don't worry, it won't happen again.' But it can."

Doctors, counselors, clergy and others in the help-professions can assist parents in protecting their children. And fathers and mothers need all the help they can get.

"Bring their lives to fulfilment in health and happiness and mercy." [TOBIT 8:17]

꠸ Make us more careful, Lord, in carrying out the responsibilities You have given us.

A ONE-WEEK COURSE in gardening changed the lives of Kenya villager Mariamu Githoni and her family.

Eight years ago, a UNICEF course taught Mariamu new methods of growing a kitchen garden. Since then, she has filled her family's five acres with 6-pound cabbages, fist-sized tomatoes, corn stalks 7-feet tall and foot-long carrots.

Mariamu recently sold 1,040 cabbages, and her regular sales of kale and carrots have paid for a cow and school fees for her children.

The course, says Mariamu, taught her about spacing, transplanting and plant diseases. Then, she says, "I started changing my method of just putting in a seed and waiting for the sun and rain and God to do the rest."

Give someone a fish and you have staved off hunger for a day. Teach someone to fish, and you have staved off hunger for a lifetime. The same goes for farming.

UNICEF—and other worthwhile agencies—are trying to do the job. They need our support.

> "Lord, when did we see You hungry and feed You, or thirsty and give You drink?"
> [MATTHEW 25:37]

~ Jesus, You fed the hungry. May we do the same.

ITH THE PRECISION, planning and purpose of Everest's conquerors, a 27-year-old toymaker climbed the 110 stories of New York's World Trade Center.

That's 1,350 feet up. A crowd gathered below and watched as George Willig, an experienced mountain climber, ascended with a rope harness and clamps he had designed to fit the metal runners used for window-washing gear. Two policemen tried in vain to persuade him to join them on a window-washing scaffold lowered from the roof. But as the toymaker coolly completed his climb, their concern grew to awe. When he reached the top after a three-and-a-half hour climb, the crowd below cheered.

A city official filed a $250,000 suit against the man. The mayor settled for $1.10, a penny a storey.

Most of us have no desire for unnecessary chances, and that's probably just as well. Yet we have to give grudging admiration to such daredevil feats.

But here's a risk anyone can take. Show love—and be willing to receive it.

> "Above all these put on love, which binds everything together in perfect harmony."
>
> [COLOSSIANS 3:14]

Make us more daring in trying to do Your work in this world, Lord, without becoming reckless.

 RE YOU A DAYDREAMER? Don't feel bad, says Dr. Jerome Singer, Yale psychologist. You're in good company. Most famous people are.

Dr. Singer, author of a book titled *The Inner World of Daydreaming*, thinks daydreams should be treasured and developed. Daydreams help teenagers plan for the future. They can entertain people tired after a day's work. They can be rehearsals for future actions. They can release tension, and stimulate creativity.

"Set aside some time each day to let your fancy wander," he advises. "Put your feet up, close your eyes, and relax. Imagine yourself in a meadow and see where you go. Get in touch with your inner self... or pick out a specific problem and let your mind run over possible solutions."

Sometimes we get so hooked on achieving that we forget that "wool-gathering" or the incubation period is vital to the creative process. It can be fun, too.

Setting aside time to "just sit" can be opportunity for silent prayer as well. And we all could use that.

> "He leads me beside still waters; he restores my soul." [PSALM 23:2,3]

ẽ Keep us from getting on an eternal treadmill, Holy Spirit, and direct our hearts to higher things.

ILLEGIBLE HANDWRITING is the largest single cause of error in business.

So says Frank King, executive vice-president of the Writing Instrument Manufacturers Association. Poorly written orders, scribbled messages and bills and bookkeeping garbles are sabotaging the marketplace at the rate of $100 million a year.

And it's not only in business. "Handwriting in this country," says Mr. King, "has deteriorated to a level which makes it almost a national scandal."

Perhaps not wanting to be associated with a downhill slide, the WIMA has launched a campaign to improve matters. Those who join the campaign are asked to write, "I will try to write more clearly" on a sheet of paper and put that pledge in a prominent place.

How we communicate may not be as important as what we say. But a message that can't be deciphered might just as well remain unspoken or unwritten. It is a mark of respect to speak or write clearly and with consideration. It's also smart communication.

> "In great or small matters, do not act amiss."
> [SIRACH 5:15]

℮ᶾ   Remind us to take the time, Lord, to put our good ideas into a form that can be understood.

MORE AND MORE colleges are teaching it. Corporations and civic governments are becoming interested in it. Patsy B. Edwards considers herself a pioneer in the field: leisure counseling.

Mrs. Edwards started Constructive Leisure in Los Angeles in 1968. Clients come because they are bored, she says, or otherwise dissatisfied with their leisure life.

A high-powered executive learns to find relaxation in a craft. A matron moves into satisfying charity work. In each instance, Patsy Edwards uses a scientific approach to help her clients choose a leisure activity.

"People need to be as systematic in their decisions about their personal lives," she claims, "as they are about their professional lives ... satisfying leisure is not just something that happens."

Play, work—and even prayer—can be approached haphazardly. Or we can think and plan. You guess which approach is apt to be more successful and satisfying.

> "Many are the plans in the mind of a man, but it is the purpose of the Lord that will be established." [PROVERBS 19:21]

ᕌ   Lord, teach us to plan time wisely.

WHEN ELIOT WIGGINTON, fresh out of Cornell University, began teaching, one of his bored students set fire to the teacher's platform.

Instead of deciding he'd chosen the wrong profession, Mr. Wigginton devised a plan to get his students more involved.

"How would you like to throw away the text and put out a magazine about local (Rabun Gap, Georgia) people and the way they live?" he asked his students.

That initial idea has become the money-making *Foxfire,* a quarterly of Southern mountain folklore completely put together by the high school students. One of their anthologies hit some best seller lists.

Eliot Wigginton could have sat around complaining about the boredom of his students. Instead, he changed his approach to meet their needs. Even if he hadn't succeeded, his efforts would have been worth it.

There is a way, if we have the will. One person can make a difference. You are one person, and you can do something.

> "I try to please all men in everything I do, not seeking my own advantage but that of many."
> [1 CORINTHIANS 10:33]

ᏒᏃ   Make us more aware, Father, of what can be done instead of lamenting what can't.

E ALL have failures. *Executives' Digest* has listed some questions that can help us profit from them.

1. Can you accept the fact that you've goofed?

2. What caused the mistake? If you can't pinpoint the origin, call in someone who can supply the insight.

3. Was planning at fault? Did you make an error in judgment? Or in fact?

4. Could bad timing have been a factor?

5. Did the mistake result from poor information? Was the accuracy of the data checked?

6. Was someone else at fault? Consider this, but remember it's easy to blame others for one's own mistakes.

7. Did you bite off more than you could chew?

8. Was the launching a success and the follow-up forgotten?

9. Do you have a bias that could have interfered?

It takes effort and pain to admit mistakes.

God is Spirit. And He speaks to our spirit when we open ourselves to listen. But we need to be open.

"We all make many mistakes." [JAMES 3:2]

 e͜ Convince us, Lord, that no error is wasted if it is followed by the effort to profit by it.

BRENDA JOY MAYO'S PIONEERING research on cystic fibrosis has a special meaning for her. She is a victim of the disease herself.

The 25-year-old Ph.D. candidate in human genetics at the University of Texas hopes to determine which parent is the carrier in CF-prone families.

Finding she had CF at age 14, Brenda made her decision. She worked her way through Lamar University in Beaumont. "I had no time to waste," she says. Doctors persuaded her to forego medical school, but she now plans to enroll anyway, after earning a Ph.D.

"I'm not afraid of my fate anymore," she says, "nor of the hurt. The greatest loss in life is what dies inside us while we still live."

What hurts the most may be refusal to admit the pain in our lives or the absolute certainty of death. If we can come to terms with the worst that is likely to happen, we can be free to get on with the business of living.

If we ask, God will help us choose life.

"Choose life." [DEUTERONOMY 30:19]

Make us more honest, Lord, more confident of what, with You, we can do.

Miss America of 1958 is now Marilyn Van Derbur, company president. Her product is motivation.

After giving up her crown, Ms. Van Derbur made numerous appearances as a TV hostess. She felt a lack of challenge but the youthful audiences gave her an idea.

Today, the Marilyn Van Derbur Motivational Institute produces films designed to help teenage students to set goals in life. Married and the mother of a five-year-old daughter, the former titlist also travels to sell her films—5,000 so far.

Motivation is something she knows about. As a girl, she had a goal—to be Miss America—and by planning and determined effort she made it possible.

"The vital, successful people I have met," she says, "all had one common characteristic. They had a plan."

Living with a plan—for the long run and for the day—is an effective way to live creatively. It gives us a chance to make a difference.

> "The Lord searches all hearts, and understands every plan and thought."
> [1 CHRONICLES 28:9]

In setting our goals, Lord, may we be in tune with Your will.

Architect Richard Foster and his wife couldn't decide which of several spectacular views to choose for their home. So they built a revolving house.

The Wilton, Connecticut, house looks like a mushroom. The circular many-windowed living quarters revolves, reverses, or stops at the push of a button.

A one-and-a-half horsepower motor on a ball-bearing assembly makes it possible for all rooms to have a view of pine woods, pond and waterfall, meadows or hills.

"We couldn't decide . . ." says Mrs. Foster, of the many views, "so we incorporated all of them."

Potted plants and trees all catch the sun. Shade or sun can be chosen to cool or warm a room, to seek out a breeze or shelter from the wind.

Creative thinking can improve more than your view. It can make you more flexible in tackling the thorny problems life brings your way. And it can show new vistas of service to those around you.

Your mind's a wonderful gift. Use it.

"Blessed is the man who meditates on wisdom and who reasons intelligently."

[SIRACH 14:20]

Give me Your wisdom, Holy Spirit, at points of decision.

WE DON'T KNOW much about Bob Broadtree of Bointon, England. But we can guess a lot.

A recent news story has it that he made a parachute jump from a light plane near Bointon.

"I just put my head back," he said, "and watched the great yellow parachute open above me. It was a fantastic experience."

It was Mr. Broadtree's first jump. It was also, undoubtedly, his last. But he is glad he did it—he established a record as the world's oldest parachutist.

Bob Broadtree is 85 years old.

Some people are young at 85. Others are old at 25. One key factor in staying young at heart is openness to new experiences and ideas.

And it's possible and very useful to have that kind of youthful outlook at any age—with both feet planted firmly on the ground.

> "You did show me the path of life; in Your presence there is fullness of joy."
>
> [PSALM 16:11]

  Keep us open to what life has to offer, Holy Spirit.

Two WOMEN HAVE COMBINED very different personalities and skills to do one executive job in Binghamton, New York.

In a new approach known as "jobsharing," Pat Rehberg and Dolores Brosnan both have the title of director of the Binghamton YWCA. Each works three 9-to-5 days during the regular work week. They take turns attending night meetings. And both women have lectured on the benefits of their unique plan.

The idea, tried on a limited basis across the country, is regarded as a work alternative especially geared to women's needs. Salary, responsibilities, problems, recognition—and headaches—are shared by two people hired to fill one slot.

Many of us get "locked in" to a single way of solving a problem. If that fails, we're out of luck. Actually, by looking at difficult situations from a variety of angles, a light may go on. And that light could illuminate a lot of other lives.

"Light will shine on your ways." [JOB 22:28]

ⅇ҉   Help us when we try to be creative, Holy Spirit.

TODAY'S REFRIGERATOR does more than keep the family's food supply, says *Boston Globe* writer Margo Miller. It also is the family's messenger.

Ms. Miller says the refrigerator door's sheer vertical space is the chosen spot for youngsters' school papers, notes from family members to each other, cartoons, reminders, poems and bargain ads. With magnetized letters, it is often the first teacher of the alphabet to toddlers.

For Melissa and David Stephenson, it is the place where they post their apologies after a fight. "But we haven't had a fight in a long time," says Melissa.

The "deeper significance" of the refrigerator door as a family messenger may be the subject of some scholarly psychological article, jokes Ms. Miller.

She adds that Boston therapist Dr. Robert Brooks suggests the perfect title: "Surface as Symbol: The Refrigerator Door as Emotional Nurturant in the Family Unit."

To give real emotional nourishment, say it directly: "I'm sorry." "I love you." "That was a great job."

> "A pleasant voice multiplies friends, and a gracious tongue multiplies courtesies."
> [SIRACH 6:5]

Sometimes, Lord, the most important words are hardest to say. Help me to say them.

MOHAWK INDIAN rituals celebrate tribal belief that the universe is one big family, says spokesman Tekarontakeh.

First, tribesmen greet those present, expressing the hope for agreement while they are together. Then they thank "Mother Earth" for all things, from blades of grass to tall trees, and for carrying out the Creator's will.

They thank "Grandmother Moon" for the cycles of women, water, childbirth and seed planting. And they thank the "Grandfathers, the four winds," for the rain and snow. "Brother Sun" is thanked for strength and light, and the "Cousins, the stars" for dew, plants, food, medicine and beauty.

Finally, says Tekarontakeh, they thank the Creator, but feel no need to ask Him for more because "if one little thing were missing, none of us would be here."

A sense of gratitude can deepen our appreciation of all things. How often do we thank God our Father for the blessings He has given to us.

"The blessings of your Father are mighty."
[GENESIS 49:26]

é̀ Keep us mindful, Father, that You are the Source of all things.

CLASSROOMS ARE AS BIG as America's wilderness for students of Diana and Michael Cohen's Trailside School.

Each year, Trailside's school bus roams all over America, while the Cohens and Frank and Beth Trocco teach widely varied accredited subjects to 20 high school level students. Wilderness life is their learning tool.

With advanced degrees in guidance, natural science, conservation and English, the Cohens and Troccos conduct America's first "ecology expedition school."

School is seven days a week, 24 hours a day, says Michael. "We spend days on a mountain, taking America apart by questioning—learning geology, human ecology, astronomy. It's catching on. We're not the only ones bringing a class to order in a national park anymore."

If you look at things from the proper perspective, the whole world can be one big visual aid. The right kind of teacher can turn it into a lesson kids will never forget.

Ask God to send us more such teachers.

"Speak and teach rightly."   [LUKE 20:21]

❧   Holy Spirit, guide teachers as they shape young minds.

WHEN HIS FAMILY LOST everything in World War II, Austrian teenager Walter Stolle reacted with a wild idea—to take off on the longest bike ride ever made. He did. It took him 18 years.

First, the youth left for England, became a citizen and spent five years preparing for his journey. "I read all kinds of travel books," he says, "and I learned languages." He speaks seven.

After getting in shape by bicycling the length of Britain, the young adventurer set out on January 25, 1959, with a 44-pound pack, half of which was photographic equipment. He replaced worn-out or stolen bikes 11 times. He crossed oceans by freighter, liner and plane, travelling 400,000 miles in all.

To finance the trip, Mr. Stolle gave 2,600 lectures and slide shows at $100 a performance. Now back in England, he is writing a book. "What I have learned and seen," he says, "nobody can take away from me."

The cost in material things is a small price to pay when it leads to enrichment of your inner self.

"Apply your mind to My knowledge."
[PROVERBS 22:17]

Help me, Jesus, to follow Your life closely so that I may know what is really important in mine.

A STUDY OF 10,000 EMPLOYEES led the Carnegie Institute to this conclusion: Only 15 percent of success is due to technical skill. The remaining 85 percent is due to personal development.

Here are the traits 70 large corporations listed as most important in business success:

1. Ability to work cooperatively with others;
2. Ability to communicate;
3. Enthusiasm - initiative and drive;
4. Appearance - neatness and proper dress;
5. Balance - especially emotional balance, personality balance;
6. Leadership - the kind that others are eager to follow, not compelled to obey.

Success—whatever its causes—is usually no accident. It results from thought, hard work and more than a little courage.

The next time you're tempted to sit around complaining "If only ..." try saying "Why don't I?" It will make a big difference.

> "Arise and be doing! The Lord be with you!"
> [1 CHRONICLES 22:16]

&ppp; Father, help us to realize how much power we have to make a difference.

When Terry Wilfong, 12, applied for a summer job at the St. Louis Museum, he signed his name in English and in hieroglyphics. He got the job.

He impressed assistant curator Thelma Stockho with his perceptive praise for the museum's Egyptian collection and his observation of some errors in descriptions of the ancient treasures. She put him to work as a volunteer guide and authorized him to correct the museum's mistakes.

"I became interested in Egyptology," says Terry, "after I saw a picture of King Tut in a book." Within a year he had taught himself to read and write the 5,000-year-old language.

Now entering ninth grade, the young scholar's goal is to become a curator in a museum.

Unlike Terry Wilfong, many people never choose what they want to be. Instead, they drift. Enjoy the freedom to be the person you can be. Help others to experience that freedom. It's a God-given right. Don't forfeit it.

"Where the Spirit of the Lord is, there is freedom." [2 CORINTHIANS 3:17]

Give us the awareness, Father, of our freedom and our responsibility to become what You have created us to be.

THE SYLLABUS OF A NEW SCHOOL includes basic floor acrobatics and introduction to aerial skills. It's the New York School for Circus Arts, an institution that trains circus performers.

Paul Binder, 34, and his partner, both jugglers, returned from a tour with a French circus and decided to start a school to revive "an art form nearly lost in America." In large American circuses, says Mr. Binder, 90 percent of the major acts are imported.

There are classes for aspiring professionals of all ages, an after-school program for children from 8 to 18 and a workshop for gifted children.

"We will not teach clowning," says Mr. Binder. "It is not . . . so easily taught."

Whether it's circus arts, folk crafts or home cooking, our society is in danger of losing the personal art form, the skill carefully handed down from one practitioner to another.

If you have a skill, pass it along to one other person. It's a way to multiply good things.

> "As each has received a gift, employ it for one another." [1 PETER 4:10]

ᏋᏋ Jesus, show us ways to share with one another.

A WEALTHY YOUNG MAN had an experience which was the climax of his spiritual struggle and his own destiny.

The richly dressed Francis, son of a prosperous merchant of 13th century Assisi, rode his horse one day on the Umbrian Plain. As his horse shied he saw the sight he most feared. A leper stood before him. But he fought down his loathing, dismounted and gave the man money.

Suddenly Francis was filled with love and kissed the leper's hand, then embraced him. In that moment he knew where his heart was—with the Man of Nazareth whose love for every person has transforming power.

He mounted his horse and returned to Assisi with joy. It was the beginning of a life of material poverty and spiritual riches in which he would be joined by hundreds of men and women of his time, and millions right up to today.

We can receive the gift of love that God holds out to us if we let go of what we are clutching. It could be fear or greed or self-importance—whatever keeps us from being open to Him and to others.

  "If anyone has the world's goods and sees his brother in need, yet closes his heart against him, how does God's love abide in him?"

          [1 JOHN 3:17]

Time MAGAZINE DID an issue on forced retirement. Letters poured in to the editor. Teresa Glazier, 69, wrote:

"Kicked out of the California educational system at 65 (she had one week's notice), I was hired by Western Illinois University...to start a remedial English program. The program is now flourishing."

Ms. Glazier went on to say that when she couldn't find a simple enough text book, she decided to write one. (The book, *The Least You Should Know About English*, sold 38,000 copies in 11 months.)

Teresa Glazier made no claim to being unusual. "I just happened to be hired by a university that does not mind my being over 65," she said, "and my book just happened to hit the market at the right time."

Ms. Glazier sounds like a person to whom things don't "just happen." She makes them happen. It's living creatively. It means refusing to accept things without question. It means asking "why?" or "why not?" It means taking part in making a world.

"Try to learn what is pleasing to the Lord."
[EPHESIANS 5:10]

ॐ   Help us, Lord, to live in such a way as to make the world a little better.

FOR 45 YEARS, Ingvald Stevens, 91, has lived alone on an island in Minnesota near the Canadian border where the temperature can plunge to 45 below.

Steve, as he is called, left Norway at 19 in 1904. After some schooling, he farmed, clerked and managed a store. Then he developed ulcers. At that point he moved to his island. For him, it's the perfect life.

A few times a year, when he needs supplies, he visits friends in the nearest town 50 miles away. He grinds his wheat, grows his vegetables, hauls water from the crystal lake. To get to the nearest mail drop, essential to his lively correspondence and to his book supply, he travels eight miles by boat or on skis.

"I love solitude," the old Norwegian told a visitor, his voice raspy from disuse. "I love the wilderness. I love the wildlife." He feels he hasn't quit the real world, he has discovered it.

To discover in what situation we "come alive," and to recognize that it's different for each person, is to give us and our world vitality.

> "I am the way, the truth, and the life."
>
> [JOHN 14:6]

    Lord, may I hear Your voice deep within me telling me the way.

Paul Sahlin's "pipe dream" has brought music to his family, friends and neighbors in Burlingame, California.

Mr. Sahlin, a personnel manager for a sugar company, recently finished building in his home a 1,332-pipe organ begun in 1974.

The handmade console is oak and walnut with ivory keys. He has made 26 ranks of pipes ranging from an inch to 17 feet, made of pine and poplar, a tin-lead alloy and polished copper. They fill a living room alcove, a stairway and the entire attic loft.

A self-taught organ builder, Mr. Sahlin worked evenings, weekends and two summer vacations to complete his dream. His inaugural recital, performed by a church organist, drew 44 guests. Neighbors ask him to open a window when he plays in the evenings.

"Yes, I do intend to share this with my friends and neighbors," he said. "It's going to be a happy time."

We feel good when we accomplish something, even better when that accomplishment brings joy to others.

> "Those who plan good have joy."
> [PROVERBS 12:20]

ક Help me, Lord, to use my ability to make those around me a little happier.

ORVILLE KELLY, whose own illness led him to start Make Today Count, an organization for the terminally ill, suggests to those afflicted:

- Talk about the illness. If it is cancer, call it cancer.
- Consider each day as another day of life, a gift from God to be enjoyed as fully as possible.
- Realize that life is never going to be perfect. It wasn't before and it won't be now.
- Pray! It is your strength, not a sign of weakness.
- Learn to live with your illness instead of considering yourself dying from it.
- Put your friends and relatives at ease. If you don't want pity, don't ask for it.
- Make arrangements for funerals, wills, etc., and make certain your family understands them.
- Set new goals; realize your limitations. The simple things of life can become the most enjoyable.
- Discuss your problems with your family as they occur. The problem is not yours alone.

"A man's spirit will endure sickness; but a broken spirit who can bear?"

[PROVERBS 18:14]

ᥱᢒ   Lord, help me to live with You, and to die with You. I need never feel alone.

Sam Levenson has been, and is, many things: schoolteacher, guidance counselor, comedian, author and philosopher. He tells this story of his classroom days:

"One day, somebody threw me the question, 'What is love?' I said, 'I'll tell you the truth. I cannot tell you what it is but I can tell you when it ain't.'

"I said, 'You know when it ain't, don't you?' And the kids' heads went 'yes.'

"'And you know when brotherhood ain't, don't you? And you know when compassion ain't, don't you?'

"And, boy, they understood."

Who wouldn't love to have had Sam Levenson for a teacher! No preaching or ponderous explanations. Instead, the challenge of being asked to think.

For parents, teachers, anyone working with the young, a good way to involve a youngster in finding the answer is to make him or her a partner.

They will thrive on that boost to self-esteem.

"Teach me good judgment and knowledge, for I believe in Your commandments."

[PSALM 119:66]

ℰ   May we learn to teach, Jesus, as You taught, with love and patience.

An OLD REFRAIN laments, "For want of a nail, the shoe was lost; for want of the shoe, the horse was lost." And eventually rider, battle and war were lost, because of the nail.

The modern version of that crucial loss took place at the Tennessee Valley Authority's Brown's Ferry nuclear power plant. A worker let a protective galosh fall into a reactor. It threatened to plug the cooling system so vital to safety in the plant.

Until it had proof that the shoe had disintegrated, the T.V.A. kept the plant closed down. The shutdown lasted for 17 days and cost $2.8 million.

In commenting on the event, *The New York Times* drew several possible morals. Among them: "The more sophisticated man's inventions, the more damaging his inattentions."

The most sophisticated of man's inventions are not as complicated as God's masterwork, the human person. Our inattentions to each other can do irreparable damage. But what little things can make a person flourish! Try some.

"Let us not love in word or speech but in deed and in truth." [1 JOHN 3:18]

Help me, Lord, always to do or say the loving thing that can make a difference in someone's life.

To YOUNGSTERS who seem to be "climbing walls," the Connecticut Wilderness School offers rock-climbing.

The 19-day wilderness course is the core of one of Connecticut's most innovative juvenile corrections programs, "a physical route," says director John Flood, "to change a mental attitude."

"What we try to do," says Mr. Flood, "... is to give these kids a chance to prove to themselves that they can do what they want to do. The whole idea ... is that your limits are a lot further than you ever imagined."

Since its start in 1974, some 350 youths, aged 15 to 22, have taken part in the program. A follow-up involves student, school and referring agency. The number of repeat offenders has dropped from 40 percent to 11 percent.

"Once you begin to develop a sense of self-value in these youngsters," says a youth services official, "... you begin to have some basis for working with them."

Self-esteem is crucial to growth. Help children to value themselves by showing that you value them as persons. Offer them chances to test their limits.

> "We may be mutually encouraged by each other's faith, both yours and mine."
>
> [ROMANS 1:12]

ୡ   Lord, help us always to be aware of the value of a person, young or old.

Two Norwegian adventurers set out recently on a 31-foot fishing vessel to recreate the nearly 1,000-year-old voyage of Viking explorer Leif Ericson.

Ragnar Thorseth, 27, and Alf Motubakk, 38, followed the Viking's presumed route to North America. They lived in the same style as the Norsemen had, but their boat had an engine.

"I'm even more curious to know what made Leif Ericson go," says Mr. Thorseth. "They knew nothing in his lifetime—they thought the earth was a pancake. Even with our equipment it is difficult sometimes, and they had nothing but sail and oar. I really admire their courage."

The Vikings had more than sail and oar. They had faith that their journey would succeed if they made the effort. They had courage to brave the unknown. They had hope that tomorrow can be different from today.

Do you and I have these traits going for us? Tackle a challenge today.

"Put out into the deep."   [LUKE 5:4]

ε̃   Father, give us courage as we face each new day.

Y OUR IDEA can change the world—if it lives to grow up. Mike LeFan, in *Toastmaster* magazine, suggests "ways to keep your brainchild from becoming an orphan":

● The first and most crucial step is to convince people that a need exists, and your idea fills it.

● Look at the problem and your solution from the point of view of others.

● Present your idea thoughtfully, clearly and briefly.

● Work beforehand with a few people who can support your position.

● Don't oversell. Don't tear down others' ideas, or dwell on past failures.

● Finally, summarize your idea in writing, to organize and clarify it for yourself and others.

A good idea is one thing. Getting it accepted and acted on is another. God's truth is in your hands. Treat it lovingly. Make it effective.

"Rather, speaking the truth in love, we are to grow up in every way." [EPHESIANS 4:15]

℮ Jesus, make us effective instruments of Your truth.

WINNING TOYS on carnival midways is not just sport for Johnny Glaze of Sherwood, Arkansas. Kids depend on it.

Each summer and fall Mr. Glaze, known as the "Robin Hood of the Midway," follows the state and county fair circuit, winning hundreds of teddy bears and kewpie dolls. These go to the Arkansas Children's Hospital and the Salvation Army for presents for children.

"A lot of people will go to fairs and win these things, then take them home and just throw them away," he says. "But the kids really appreciate the toys. They have a shelf at Children's Hospital lined with these things. When they take kids out of surgery, they'll bring them by and let them pick one out."

Johnny Glaze is good at winning carnival prizes. And he turned it to good use. Kids in the hospital benefit from his unique skill.

You have special talents, too. How can you use them for others?

> "We know that in everything God works for good with those who love Him."
>
> [ROMANS 8:28]

ಆ Jesus, You were always helping people. Show us ways to follow You.

WRITING POETRY is a vital part of police detective Arthur Munoz's night shift in San Antonio, Texas.

Officer Munoz, 50, a 20-year police veteran, has written poems for 35 years—on note pads, assignment sheets and paper napkins.

"I'm glad I've done all this writing," he says. "This is something to let you break out. It's cheaper than a psychiatrist's couch."

Officer Munoz is now looking for a publisher. "I want to bring this out: the police image is not what people think it is."

Most "images" are just that—surface impressions that may have little to do with what people are really like.

The most exciting discovery we may ever make is that of finding the real person of others under the layers of "images."

> "It is He who will give insight to your mind, and your desire for wisdom will be granted."
> [SIRACH 6:37]

ᏋᎦ Deepen our perception, Lord, and help us to see the goodness in the hearts of family and friends.

Sixty "BLUE COLLAR WOMEN" of Brooklyn, New York, founded their own two-year college—the first of its kind.

The women, chapter members of the National Congress of Neighborhood Women, are from working class, low and fixed income ethnic groups. They work on issues like education, health, housing, legal services and welfare.

Sponsored by LaGuardia Community College of CUNY, the new school has classrooms in several neighborhoods, and teaches women how to become community leaders.

"I've learned more in 10 months here than I ever did any place else," says one of the students. "I've learned about politics, economics, group dynamics. I bring it home to my husband, my sister, my in-laws." Said another: "Politicians are paying attention to us."

If we are ever to get a way to handle the problems besetting our nation, it will probably come from the united efforts of people on the local level. Pray and work for greater cooperation where you live.

> "For the whole law is fulfilled in one word,
> 'You shall love your neighbor as yourself.'"
> [GALATIANS 5:14]

Inspire in us, Lord, a sense of the "here and now" as we look for ways to serve others.

CHELSEA HOUSE, a senior citizen home in Chicago, has a pool table. That's important to 91-year-old resident Frances Molitor. After all, she just took up the game and needs a place to play.

Recalling her youth, Mrs. Molitor said, "Women just didn't go into poolrooms in those days. But things are different today. Lots of people even have pool tables in their homes."

"I was just getting bored, sitting around doing nothing. I used to knit but my eyes went bad. I wanted to do something active," says Mrs. Molitor. Already a finalist in one tournament, this senior citizen says she hopes to win it next year.

Mrs. Molitor may be old in years. But she's young in spirit. Her willingness to try new things keeps her that way.

Are you open to the new, the different? It'll keep you young, no matter what the calendar says.

> "A new heart I will give you, and a new spirit I will put within you." [EZEKIEL 36:26]

ᴇᴅ Father, may we see Your hand in each new day's events.

A t GRANT JR. HIGH of Syracuse, New York, boys are learning to bake and sew, and girls are studying mechanics.

Grant was among the first schools to begin programs of boys' home economics and girls' shop.

"It's working out great," says industrial arts teacher Charles Bartlett. "The girls are doing just fine, especially in the drafting classes."

Boys, in turn, study early childhood development, nutrition, consumer education, cooking and sewing.

"Having boys in the home economics classes is different," says one teacher, whose boys are sewing sweatshirts. "The boys are very adept with the small machines."

Says principal Nick Abdo, "It's been a good experience for us all."

When we take a chance and approach people as individuals, rather than as stereotypes, it usually turns out to be a good experience for all. God didn't mass-produce us. And in cherishing individuality—our own and every one else's—we honor Him.

> "Before I formed you in the womb I knew you, and before you were born I consecrated you."
> [JEREMIAH 1:5]

Father, thank You for making me a unique, unrepeatable person.

ONLY 10 PERCENT of Americans ever write to their Congressmen, says Arizona Representative Morris Udall. Stressing that writing to Congressmen is vital to the democratic process, he gives these pointers:

● Address letters to "Hon. _____ House Office Bldg., Washington, D.C. 20515," or "Senator _____ Senate Office Bldg., Washington, D.C. 20515."

● Identify the issue, with the bill number.

● Be brief. Type or write clearly. Limit letters to important issues.

● Write your own letters, your own opinions.

● Detail reasons you are taking a stand.

● Be constructive. Share your expertise.

● Don't threaten, and do say "well done" when praise is deserved.

War, poverty and justice are some of the vital concerns of humanity. As citizens and as children of God we have the obligation to share in the decision making they involve. That's one way to love our neighbor. Writing a letter is one way almost anyone can help.

> "I will set my eyes upon them for good . . . I will build them up, and not tear them down."
> [JEREMIAH 24:6]

ẽé   May I ask, Lord, not "why don't 'they' do something about the world's ills," but "why don't I . . .?"

WHAT'S SO SPECIAL about jumping rope? Try 44 children at the same time.

Volunteers from the fourth, fifth and sixth grades of St. Victor's parish elementary school in Monroe, Wisconsin, recently broke a world's record.

After a week's practice, all 44 managed to jump a 100-foot rope five times without a miss. The previous mark of four jumps had been set by a mere 35 youngsters in Lorain, Ohio.

Louis Daniels, principal of St. Victor's, was one of the rope turners. It had been his idea. "They yelled, shouted and danced," said Mr. Daniels. "It was like they had won the World Series."

"It wasn't really hard," said 11-year-old Angie Hall. "It was just tricky getting everyone jumping at the same time."

A lot could be accomplished—in industry, government, homelife, and all kinds of places—if we could get more people jumping at the same time. Where can you promote cooperation toward worthwhile goals?

"Every one helps his neighbor." [ISAIAH 41:6]

  May we realize, Jesus, the power of working together to change the world.

Two AVID READERS found themselves marooned without books on an island in New York City.

When Herman Reade, 70, and his wife, Dorothy, moved to newly developed Roosevelt Island in the East River, they found there was no library.

So the Reades started a public library, pioneer style. They began with a small rent-free room, the encouragement of their neighbors and the cast-off volumes of those who had moved from larger to smaller living space. Now they have 500 members, 14,000 volumes and a 30-foot square office that is too small.

"Everything in our lives has been aiming toward this," says Dorothy Reade. They are so busy they have little time to read, but they love it. "Here we are, ordinary citizens," she says, "arranging our own library."

Often it's the "ordinary citizen" who sees a need, understands best how to fill it and gets things going. There may be an important job to be done right now.

"Excel in all that you do."   [SIRACH 33:22]

    Help me, Lord, to take responsibility instead of leaving everything to "them."

YOUNG LAWYERS in a dozen states are volunteering their services to help parolees make good.

The effort, based on one-to-one contact between lawyer and parolee, eases the load on state parole officers. Not a legal aid program, it focuses on employment and landlord problems, giving the new parolee "somebody who's going to talk to him, provide him some assistance at reassimilating into society. It's almost a big brother program," says David Crossland, III, Georgia's state coordinator.

Now underway in Maryland, Illinois, Florida, New Jersey, Missouri, Colorado, Washington, California, Virginia, Ohio, Mississippi and Georgia, it has lowered recidivism from 40 percent to two percent in some areas.

Doctor, lawyer or Indian chief, each of us helps weave the delicate fabric of society. Helping parolees is one positive way. Somewhere—in your town, on your block, in your home—someone needs what you have to give. Don't withhold it.

"Do not withhold good from those to whom it is due, when it is in your power to do it."
[PROVERBS 3:27]

෫ Jesus, You came among us as "One who serves." May Your example move us to act.

IN THE WORLD in general, there has been more rain. Crops are better. But people are still hungry.

And the ranks of those combating hunger are growing. In the United States, there are several hundred groups in the movement. Joseph Collins and Frances M. Lappe, authors of *Food First*, contend that the root causes are not droughts, backwardness or overpopulation.

The rich countries of the world, say the authors, and the rich elite and multinational corporations in poor countries are monopolizing the best farmland.

We eat more than we need, they add, importing food from countries where people go hungry.

Seek government action, urge Mr. Collins and Ms. Lappe, to drop programs encouraging such policies. "We don't expect to see an improvement overnight... we see ourselves as part of a long historical process."

To be part of that process is to take our part in making the world better than we found it, to take part in creation itself. God gives us life and talents. Let's give thanks and give our efforts.

> "But if any one has the world's goods and sees his brother in need, yet closes his heart against him, how does God's love abide in him?"
> [1 JOHN 3:17]

We thank you, Father, for our abundance. May we make it possible for others to share it.

A 10-YEAR CAMPAIGN by the World Health Organization has dropped smallpox deaths from two million to only seven cases in just 11 years.

In the past year, the only known victims of smallpox in the entire world were seven people in Ethiopian desert villages. WHO believes that these are the last cases of the disease. If no new cases are discovered within two years, WHO will declare smallpox officially conquered. The organization began its worldwide campaign in 1966 when epidemics wiped out two million men, women and children.

While criticism is leveled at the United Nations for what it is not doing, or has done badly, credit is certainly due for what it has accomplished.

If people of different countries can work together to wipe out disease, there is also hope that war can some day be similarly done away with.

Support all constructive efforts to demonstrate our global solidarity and interdependence. There are ways to "light candles" in your community, nation and world.

> "If we walk in the light ... we have fellowship with one another." [1 JOHN 1:7]

Remind us, Jesus, that we are together on our small planet, and that we need each other.

Three contemporary women calling themselves the Elizabethan Trio wanted to know if women were producing quality work in the arts 400 years ago.

What musicians Laurette Goldberg, Anna Carol Dudley and Rella Lossy found was that women were producing first rate plays, music and novels centuries ago. This despite the fact that many works remained unknown and others were destroyed.

In Elizabethan England, women thought it immodest to publish their work. Ms. Lossy said that women during those times were probably destroying work as good as their male counterparts' because it was "socially unacceptable" to publish it.

It's good to remember that women, men, children—all of us—have something to offer, something creative we can add to the quality of life for everyone.

What can you do to unlock the powers God has given you? Why not start today? This could be your day!

> "No one after lighting a lamp covers it with a vessel, or puts it under a bed, but puts it on a stand, that those who enter may see the light."
> [LUKE 8:16]

ᕓ   Father, show us how to tap our potential and spark others to do so.

Iт's HARD TO SAY "I love you." Have you noticed? The reasons could be fear: of rejection, of displaying one's feelings, of moving off the comfortable "kidding" level into a deeper relationship.

So says New York psychiatrist Dr. Frederick Flach. Doctor Flach points out that the best way "is to use the words along with some tangible evidence."

Such evidence might be a gesture, an act or a gift which show that you have given thought to what the person would like and to what the person is like.

"The definition of love in the dictionary," says Dr. Flach, "is 'to care,' and you've got to show and tell someone that you do care every day."

There are many ways to say "I love you." Sometimes we say the words. Sometimes we act in a caring way. Best is when words and meaning go together. When's the last time you said "I love you" and meant it?

"Let us love one another; for love is of God."
[1 JOHN 4:7]

ᐱᓐ   Help us, Jesus, make everything we say express concern for others.

As HALLOWEEN approaches, children start thinking about costumes and treats. Adults shop for supplies to have on hand when the doorbell rings. A nutrition expert is concerned about what happens next.

"Our children are not being treated on Halloween night," says Dr. Harold Rosenberg. "They are being tricked."

He says the sugar consumed in candy and cookies not only erodes children's teeth but, in large quantities, affects their ability to think clearly, lowers their energy level and causes greater excitability.

Dr. Rosenberg suggests some alternatives for treat bags: Fruit, homemade cookies sweetened with honey, or a non-food treat like a small toy or comic book.

The custom of "tricks or treats" solved the problem of pranks and vandalism. Maybe now is the time to make it even better.

Stop and think. There might be a better way.

> "Do not be children in your thinking; be babes in evil, but in thinking be mature."
> [1 CORINTHIANS 14:20]

   May we be sheep, Jesus, only in the sense that You are our Shepherd.

T HE STATE OF CONNECTICUT had an important message to relay to its residents and reached a large audience by mailing it with operator license renewal blanks.

The message is from the Board of Education and Services for the Blind: "It's ability that counts."

The flyer notes that the blind are successfully employed in every job field. It goes on to answer any doubts about specific problems.

● Travel. Blind persons travel independently to and from work, recreation and community responsibilities. Special mobility courses are available if needed.

● Safety. Incidence of serious job-related accidents is considerably lower than for sighted workers.

● Insurance. With that record, it's no problem.

● Attendance. Surveys indicate blind workers equal the best attendance records and are superior in punctuality.

Prejudice against people who are handicapped is usually rooted in lack of knowledge. One way to conquer it is to get to know them as individuals.

> "You are restricted in your own affections . . . I speak to you as to children—widen your hearts also."　　　[2 CORINTHIANS 6:12,13]

eé　Help me, Father, to accept each person as unique.

THE PEACE CORPS has helped to blow sky-high the increasingly fragile stereotype of aging.

Over 346 volunteers have been 50 years old or over, three dozen between 71 and 80. The Corps, a division of the Federal Volunteer Agency, Action, actively recruits older people to serve for a minimum of two years in developing nations overseas.

Men and women with careers behind them and their children grown, receive training to help with such programs as agriculture, mathematics and science teaching, teacher-training, business and public administration in Asia, Africa and Latin America.

The agency provides transportation to and from the overseas assignment and if necessary, back home for family emergencies. Volunteers receive a monthly allowance for food, travel, rent and medical needs.

A sense of adventure, the ability and willingness to learn and the desire to help: these are characteristics of vitality. If, for ourselves and others, we are open to the possible, we can achieve a lot.

> "Sow for yourselves righteousness, reap the fruit of steadfast love." [HOSEA 10:12]

ℰ Help us, Lord, to tap the vitality within ourselves that can nourish our world.

GOOD PUBLIC RELATIONS and deep concern over air pollution helped a Pittsburgh group transform their city's air quality in just seven years.

When Pittsburgh was named one of ten U.S. cities most affected by air pollution in 1969, 43 citizens organized GASP—Group Against Smog and Pollution. Deciding on "no picketing of polluters and no screaming or emotionalism," GASP gained the support of scientists, doctors, lawyers, teachers, economists, unions and "just plain concerned citizens." Residents baked "Dirty Gerty" cookies for donation drives. GASP campaigned to upgrade the state's air-quality standards, and won the right to cross-examine industries seeking variances before the Air Quality Board.

GASP's efforts have led Allegheny County to mandate one of the strongest air-quality codes in the country. Its role now includes energy needs and resources.

Thank God we live in a country where people who care can make a difference. You're a person. Do you care enough to get involved?

"Do not be weary in well-doing."
[2 THESSALONIANS 3:13]

ε̃ Father, may we work to promote the common good.

303 / OCTOBER 30

T HE IDEA for Trick or Treat for UNICEF was born in 1949 when a minister's wife saw a live display in a Philadelphia department store starring Elsie the Cow. It dramatized UNICEF's (United Nations Children's Emergency Fund) role in getting milk to children in war-devastated Europe.

Mary Emma Allison conveyed her desire to help to her husband, a member of the Presbyterian Westminster Press. Rev. Clyde M. Allison had for two years produced Junior-Hi Kits, a project to encourage youths to use Halloween as a chance to help people in need.

For the next one, he promoted the idea of collecting, not shoes or soap as before, but money for UNICEF. On Halloween, 1950, coins started dropping into the little cartons and they have been jingling ever since—to a total of almost $50 million.

To urge young people to care about others is a good start. Helping them find concrete ways to give may require your own involvement, creativity and enthusiasm. This is teaching that works.

"Show yourself in all respects a model of good deeds." [TITUS 2:7]

ළ Help us, Father, to teach as Jesus did, by living what we preach.

BERNARD KORMAN COLLECTS hands, by the thousands. Mr. Korman, a New York cab driver and commercial artist, has made studies of the hands of passengers since 1952. With Polaroid camera and sketching materials, he is always ready to capture a permanent record of an interesting hand.

While studying art, he became fascinated with the Adam scene of Michaelangelo's Creation and with Durer's Praying Hands. "Hands make perfect portraits," he explains, "you are the only one with your hands. Driving a cab gives me all the hands I could want."

Hands the cabbie-artist has recorded include Princess Grace, Mitch Miller, Arthur Rubinstein, Jack Dempsey and dozens of other celebrities.

You don't have to be an artist to find what's unique in each person. Take time to think about your own uniqueness. Thank God for it. And value that special quality in other people.

> "I have called you friends ... I chose you and appointed you that you should go and bear fruit and that your fruit should abide."
> [JOHN 15:16]

꿈 As we grow in a sense of our own worth, Jesus, help us to appreciate the worth of others, too.

BELOW ARE THE WORDS of a man whose wife had just died. Larry Martin's eulogy for his wife, Ann, was published in the alumnae magazine of St. Mary's College, Notre Dame, Indiana.

"... Death presents a sobering and all-inclusive question: Will it matter that I was?

"... Has it mattered that Ann lived? The answer really depends on each of us here today.

"... Ann was never much involved in world movements or the great social issues. She always said: 'Why look so far afield?' In our own neighborhood are people who suffer and weep, who are cold or hungry for something; people who are sick or alone, who are mourning. There they are, looking at us and waiting.

"Ann had to answer and she's asking you to continue for her."

Each person's death can be a reminder of our own. It can be a chance to reflect on our own lives and to try, with God's help, to make them meaningful. Will it matter that you were?

> "We know that we have passed out of death into life, because we love." [1 JOHN 3:14]

℘ Help us to live fuller lives, Father, by learning from the fortunes of those around us.

CHICKEN-FEATHER COOKIES, manure-fed cattle and shellfish raised on coal-slurry waste water are some of the new products that may help solve the "garbage explosion."

University of Georgia scientists have found that 10 percent of flour in cookies can be replaced by a protein-rich feather distillate. In another experiment, putting cattle on manure-based feed is proving that steak from manure-fed steers is as tasty, wholesome and nutritious as grain-fed beef.

Protein-rich shellfish thrive on the waste water from power plants and are wholesome and edible.

As by-products become food products, scientists are beginning to see that one problem—excess garbage—may solve another—food shortage.

What sustains many scientists through endless hours of research is what keeps a lot of us going—hope. If our sights are set on goals worth seeking, the Lord will help us persevere in achieving them.

"Keep alert with all perseverance."

[EPHESIANS 6:18]

ॐ Keep us from giving up, Father, in our efforts to make a better life for ourselves and others.

THE NATION'S 17-YEAR-OLDS, just one year away from voting age, have some strange ideas about government, according to a national poll of students.

● Only 53 percent knew that each state has two Senators.

● One out of every eight believed the President is not required to obey the law.

● One out of five thought that the United States was the only country that had political parties.

But the poll of 2,500 students did show that 89 percent would vote according to their convictions.

The attitude "why bother?" is one of the secret enemies of free Government. The ignorance of those who do vote is another.

Our communities and nation depend on informed and concerned citizens. Jefferson put it like this: "The penalty of wise men who fail to vote is to live under the rule of the unwise."

> "Like the magistrate of the people, so are his officials, and like the ruler of the city, so are all its inhabitants." [SIRACH 10:2]

Don't let us become apathetic, Father, about our responsibilities in government.

It took an ancient form of transportation—the carrier pigeon—to help doctors in Devon, England, overcome delays caused by modern traffic jams.

Creep-and-crawl traffic had added hours to transporting blood and tissue samples to nearby Plymouth for urgently needed lab tests. Then someone thought of flying the samples by carrier pigeon. The light-weight samples went speedily by pigeon, and now the feathered delivery team is on a regular schedule. If the successful flights continue, other British hospitals may also turn to "pigeon power."

It is heartwarming to hear that the humble pigeon can aid the medical profession in healing and saving human lives.

God made us stewards of creation. Certainly a "fair deal" since nature and its resources are provided for our happiness and welfare.

We can give thought each day to using wisely what God has given to us.

> "It was He who created man in the beginning, and He left him in the power of his own inclination." [SIRACH 15:14]

> Lord, help me to remember that You made me a steward for my own good.

VOTING MACHINE that has everything has been invented by Barnard graduate Susan Huhn of Concord, Massachusetts.

Ms. Huhn, 35, runs an election-consulting business and has designed an electronic machine that works like a sophisticated calculator, weighs just 35 pounds and costs $2,775.

Ms. Huhn's invention is easier for the voter to operate and can detect voter errors in an instant. It has switches for up to 512 candidates or questions, and handles a ballot 32 pages long. The voter can even change his or her mind after flipping the switch.

Ms. Huhn says she developed the new machine "because I'm interested more in running good elections than in the voting machine itself."

An improved voting machine is a good idea. But remember, a voting device is only as good as the citizens who use it. Know the candidates. Study the issues. And vote—as if your freedom depends on it. It does.

"You were called to freedom, brethren."
[GALATIANS 5:13]

Jesus, let us not forget to "render to Caesar what is Caesar's."

RESEARCHERS FOUND some surprising common factors among 100 Dutch people who are still healthy in their 90's—lifetimes of poverty and hard work, two world wars and a bitter economic depression.

Drs. Sven Danner and Arend Dunning studied the life histories of the hundred nonagenarians, and found that all had been unskilled laborers and had been denied "the mixed blessings of affluence."

Only 10 percent were overweight, and only 2 percent had smoked more than an occasional cigarette. They ate less than the Dutch population as a whole, and Dr. Danner reported that the cholesterol level was "remarkably low" in the subjects studied.

It is well worth it to think of the real blessings of our lives. Money cannot buy contentment or health. But doing a job well can bring contentment and physical labor can sustain good health.

And that's real wealth.

> "And every work that he undertook ... seeking his God, he did with all his heart."
> [2 CHRONICLES 31:20]

၉ Lord, help me to do what I have to do as well as I can.

$\mathcal{S}$TUDENTS IN A GIRLS' SCHOOL in Northern Ireland have, among other activities, been cleaning windows, shining shoes, selling sweets and washing cars. Why?

As part of UNESCO's Co-Action Programme, each class chose to contribute to a Third World project. Among them were education for the handicapped in Madagascar and Malaysia and a project in the Philippines by which children acquire piglets for breeding to raise money for continuing their education.

The UNESCO program enables schools and other groups, as well as individuals, to make direct contact with the people who are actually working on the projects by use of a kind of international money order (UNUM).

The girls in the Belfast secondary school, by their own efforts, managed to raise over $2,300.

We have but one world. And the only sane choice is to learn to live as one family on this shrinking planet.

Where can you start building bridges and removing barriers?

> "I will set my eyes upon them for good...I
> will build them up, and not tear them down."
> [JEREMIAH 24:6]

ↄ̣ Jesus, teach us to love one another.

HEN ETHEL CROW's friend "Chunky" died, she had the remains enshrined on her front lawn in Middletown, Pennsylvania. "Chunky" was a car.

The 1963 Chevrolet Nova had 230,000 miles on it when it finally gave out. Unwilling to junk the faithful vehicle, the woman had it squeezed into a one-ton metal block.

"I grew so attached to that car," she explains. "It never let me down. It saw me through thick and thin, ice and snow, the worst weather imaginable."

Recalled Ethel's husband Bob, "I remember one Christmas Eve we had snow that was thigh-deep. Bulldozers couldn't get through, but old Chunky moved and got Edith home that night with the trunk and back seat loaded with Christmas presents."

Anything that lives up to expectations—whether a car, a pet or another human being—deserves our appreciation. What do you and I look for in others? Are we willing to put forth the same on their behalf?

"We give thanks to God always for you all."
[1 THESSALONIANS 1:2]

Give us the sense to be grateful, Holy Spirit, for the good things that come our way.

Benny Nabors doesn't think his job is particularly dangerous, but his wife does. The first time she saw him at work, she fainted.

Mr. Nabors, a steeplejack-painter in Lavonia, Georgia, was getting into a hanging chair to begin painting the underside of a 157-foot water tank when his wife drove up.

"My wife stepped out of the car and fainted," he recounted. "I had to climb all the way back down. I told the children, 'Don't you ever bring your mama back out on the job site.'"

Mr. Nabors, 47, has never been hurt, but did have one close call in Savannah, Georgia. Falling backward inside a huge water tank, he was grabbed by a fellow worker a split second before he would have plummeted to the empty tank's bottom.

What would be dangerous for me might be "duck soup" for you. Much depends on natural ability and experience. What do we do best? What are our real strengths? Do we use them?

> "On the day I called, You did answer me, my strength of soul You did increase."
> [PSALM 138:3]

ᥱ᷉ Grant us the power of Your spirit, Lord, in all the events of our lives.

A PASTOR FINALLY realized a dream.

It was 25 years ago that Reverend Tom Bagby founded St. Martin's Episcopal Church in Houston. He has built it into one of the largest Episcopal parishes in the United States. His vestrymen wanted to honor him with a gift.

A trip to the Holy Land? A Tom Bagby chair at a seminary? No, he would like a little wayside chapel for anyone in need to come, 24 hours a day. This was his dream. "The crises that affect people's lives," he said, "don't necessarily come between 8 a.m. and 5 p.m."

So they built the chapel, a glass-walled enclosure with pews of stone and a small granite altar. A large cross outside is floodlit for evening visitors.

"It's a special place," says Reverend Bagby, "where anyone may pray or offer thanks—a quiet and unique place for anyone seeking the peace of God."

We can find God's peace in a chapel, in solitude anywhere, in the silence of our hearts. We can find it, too, with a person. You could be that person for someone else.

> "Let him seek peace and pursue it."
> [1 PETER 3:11]

May I have Your peace in my heart, Lord, so that it may be there for someone in need today.

Smiles brighten the assembly line of a manufacturing plant in Michigan City, Indiana.

Sullair Corporation produces air compressors under an unusual management strategy. Employees vote in groups on their hours. Most choose 10 hours a day, four days a week. Breaks at Sullair are unsupervised; there are no plant foremen, no time clocks.

"No boss can determine the production of a worker," says Don Hoodes, 49, president and founder of the 10-year-old company. "Everyone has to work at his own pace." Each year, employees get an extra month's salary in profit-sharing.

How does it work? Employees outproduce their United States competitors three to one. Absenteeism is near zero. "If people have the right motivation, you get high productivity," claims Mr. Hoodes.

A management approach like Sullair's takes a lot of trust in people. But, come to think about it, if you can't trust people, whom can you trust?

"Kindness and truth shall meet; justice and peace shall kiss."   [PSALM 85:10]

ℰ   Father, You trust us; May we trust each other.

ROBERT LOUIS STEVENSON GAVE to a little girl the gift of a deed which reads as follows:

"In consideration that Miss Annie H. Ide, daughter of H.C. Ide, in the State of Vermont, U.S.A., was born out of all reason on Christmas Day, and is therefore out of all justice denied the consolation and profit of a proper birthday . . .

"And considering that I have obtained an age when I have no further use for a birthday of any description . . .

"I do hereby transfer to the said Annie H. Ide all and whole my rights and privileges in the 13th day of November, to have, hold, exercise and enjoy the same in the customary manner, by sporting of fine raiment, eating of rich meats, and receipt of gifts, compliments, and copies of verse . . ."

Annie Ide kept this birthday all of her life and read the Deed of Gift aloud each November 13th, finally willing it to a favorite niece.

Thoughtfulness. Its expression can be so simple—if only we stop, look—and love.

"Be kind to one another."   [EPHESIANS 4:32]

❧   Jesus, help us to be more thoughtful.

ALL THE WORLD TRIES to cope with noise, says author R. Murray Schafer, and history shows that noise pollution has always been a problem. Schafer's book *The Tuning of the World* gives these fascinating facts:

- Julius Caesar banned all wagon traffic in Rome between sunset and sunrise.
- A Babylonian king called for divine punishment of noise-makers.
- Moscow is the quietest city in the world, with only 17 horn blasts in a nine-hour weekday period.
- Cairo is the noisiest city, with 1,150 horn blasts in a like period.
- Hong Kong's main noise complaints are over the clashing of mah jong tiles.
- Bonn, West Germany, restricts carpet beating from 8 a.m. to noon, with an extra three hours of quiet on Friday.

Noise isn't just annoying. It's a hazard to mental and physical health. What can you do to lower the volume?

"Lead a quiet and peaceable life, godly and respectful in every way."   [1 TIMOTHY 2:2]

Lord, step up our efforts to increase the peace and quiet around us.

PRISON HAS BECOME home for 65-year-old Robert Ransom.

Described as a model prisoner and parolee, Mr. Ransom returned to prison in North Carolina after being released because he couldn't get work or government financial help. He suffers with terminal lung cancer and could find no way to support himself on the outside.

Mr. Ransom, who has no family in North Carolina, had been subsisting on $46 worth of food stamps a month while living in a shack without indoor plumbing. Parole officers decided the only way to help him get regular meals, care and medical attention was to return him to prison.

"I didn't mind coming back here and I don't mind going if it's for the better," he says.

Home may be where you hang your hat. But it's also usually where you can expect to be taken care of. For some, that's an unattainable dream.

Are you grateful for your home and the people in it? Could you open your home to others?

"I was a stranger and you welcomed me."
[MATTHEW 25:35]

Jesus, remind us of those who, like You, have nowhere to lay their head.

WHILE SOME PEOPLE might consider Harold Peterson "disabled," two would-be robbers found out otherwise.

A one-legged watchman for a Brooklyn used car lot, Mr. Peterson, 54, was confronted by two holdup men demanding money. He swung his crutch, knocking the weapon from one startled gunman's hand. He grabbed the gun and fired two shots, wounding both the thugs. Then he called the police.

The men were taken to a nearby Brooklyn hospital, where both were charged with robbery.

It's too bad we can't call a halt to the use of the words "disabled" or "handicapped." At least, thinking of ourselves and others in more positive terms is closer to the truth than focusing on limitations.

There are certain things each of us can do and things we can't. What God expects, and what our sense of self-worth requires, is that we do our best. Anyone who does that is "able."

"For in due season we shall reap, if we do not lose heart." [GALATIANS 6:9]

Make us more mindful, Jesus, of the need to be positive, to have hope.

THERE'S A SPECIAL MAGIC in the feeling of a child for an animal.

The Green Chimneys School, a state-supported facility for troubled children, uses that magic for healing. At the Brewster, New York, school, a major therapeutic tool is its farm.

The children are responsible for care of the animals, and they feel at home in the midst of the moos, bahs, squeals and whinnies.

They act as guides to visiting youngsters. And program director Cathy Setterlin, speaks of community-oriented plans such as a farm festival and involvement with local 4-H clubs—all links to people.

"Animals," says a 13-year-old boy at Green Chimneys, "just give you less problems than people."

Perhaps children feel the simple acceptance of an animal, and are nourished by it. It seems such a little thing—to accept a child as he or she is, to trust the inborn source of growth in a person God created. So easy any of us can do it.

"And He took them (children) in His arms and blessed them." [MARK 10:16]

🌿 Give us the wisdom, Father, to let children grow.

IF YOU ARE PREGNANT and you smoke, your unborn baby is smoking too. Effects on the baby can be drastic, according to the American Lung Association.

• A pregnant woman who smokes two packs a day blocks off 40 percent of the unborn baby's oxygen.

• Babies of smoking mothers can be born addicted to nicotine, suffering withdrawal symptoms for months.

• Infants of smoking mothers may show chronic carbon monoxide intoxication.

• More babies of smoking mothers die in the first month.

• Smoking increases risks of premature birth and spontaneous abortion, impairs the heart rate, blood pressure, oxygen supply and acid balance of the baby.

• The placenta can filter out thousands of harmful substances, but it cannot filter out nicotine.

The responsibility that pregnant mothers have for the life and health of their unborn child underlies the duties each of us has for the welfare of others. Is that a charge we take seriously—and act on?

> "You did form my inward parts, you did knit me together in my mother's womb."
> [PSALM 139:13]

℘ Instill in each of us, Holy Spirit, a reverence for all human life, from womb to deathbed.

ERIC LEEK USED TO have fantasies about being a millionaire. Now he can live like one.

The 27-year-old hairstylist won the biggest lottery prize in the nation's history—$1,776 a week for life in New Jersey's "1776 Instant Lottery Drawing."

The money is coming in all right. So are marriage proposals, business offers and requests for interviews. Complications have forced the winner to move and get an unlisted phone number.

The lucky winner has bought a Jaguar, another dream come true. And he has taken a couple of trips. He cuts hair only now and then, "to keep his hand in." But he hasn't figured out what to do with his life. It's not the way he thought it would be. "There's nothing more powerful than the almighty dollar," says Mr. Leek, "but all it really gives you is a false sense of happiness."

Beyond a certain necessary minimum, our lives are determined by something other than the size of our bank account. What we are and what we do counts for more than how much we have.

> "If riches increase, set not your heart on
> them."   [PSALMS 62:10]

    Keep our eyes focused on doing what You want, Lord, and help us fulfill our potential.

A T A TIME OF SOARING costs, a San Francisco heart doctor has invented a life-saving device that costs $20.

"You could call it a disposable EKG," says Dr. Herman Uhley of San Francisco. His machine is about the size of a pocket calculator. A patient can build it with components available at radio equipment stores. Little knowledge of electronics is needed.

Here's how it works: The machine converts electricity produced by the heart into a high-pitched sound. When the patient feels a chest pain, he can monitor his own heart rhythm and relay it to the doctor or hospital over the telephone. An electrocardiogram machine at the other end decodes the tone and the patient is told whether he should come to the hospital.

Dr. Uhley didn't patent the device. Published instructions are available to any patient who needs it.

You have to admire someone who puts special skills at the service of the public. More of us could do that. Why we don't tells something about ourselves. With God's help, it can be different.

"Do good and share what you have."

[HEBREWS 13:16]

Father, help us to look for ways we can share Your love.

ℬARBARA COYLE'S SMILE foiled a holdup in Amherst, New York.

The clerk looked up from her cash register to see a man in a black ski mask, gun poised. He demanded money. The mask made him appear to be smiling. Then she spotted a man in a car outside. He seemed to be smiling, too. So she smiled back.

"A joke," she thought, and smiled broadly at the holdup man. He brandished the gun, but she only smiled more brightly. Unnerved, he fled.

The man outside ran in, asking if something was wrong. He couldn't figure out, he said, why she had returned his smile. Only then did Ms. Coyle realize the man with the gun had been serious.

At last report, police were still looking for the would-be bandits.

More smiles might make life more pleasant. But smiling won't make people more honest. That's a conscious choice each of us must make. Have you made that choice? Do you abide by it?

> "Do not depend on dishonest wealth, for it will not benefit you in the day of calamity."
> [SIRACH 5:8]

ℯₑ Lord, help us to be honest.

For 18 YEARS, Chicago Fire Department's Battalion 22 has enjoyed a cake, inscribed with "Thanks again to the men of the Chicago Fire Department for saving my life."

Charles Thinger says it's the least he can do for the men who pulled him from a fire May 23, 1959.

"I'm most indebted to the firemen," he says. He would have "been a goner" without them.

"It started out as a kind of personal way to say thank you to the men," he says. Though all the original crew have moved on, he still brings the cake.

"It doesn't make any difference that the original firemen aren't here anymore, it's a symbolic thing," claims Mr. Thinger, "honoring all the firemen in the city—and everywhere in the country."

Gratitude—how precious and how rare. A lot of people have contributed to making your life more pleasant and richer.

When's the last time you said "thanks?"

"Give thanks in all circumstances."
[1 THESSALONIANS 5:18]

ed   Holy Spirit, may we show gratitude more spontaneously.

BECAUSE OF A SENSITIVE nose, Paul Angstadt walked over 85,000 miles in 25 years.

Mr. Angstadt's job with the Sun Company was sniffing for leaks in the firm's gasoline pipeline from Deer Path to Allentown, Pennsylvania. He kept a log for 25 years prior to his retirement.

The log showed that he walked 14 miles a day through rain, snow, and summer heat, wearing out 117 pairs of shoes and 372 pairs of socks. During his daily treks, he chewed 6,318 packs of tobacco.

Now 70 and retired, Mr. Angstadt never missed a day of work because of illness.

Mr. Angstadt obviously liked his job. We can take a lesson from his diligence and apply it to things of the spirit. We can persevere in doing good—conscienciousness at work, care about obligations to our family. And it will help our spiritual health, too.

"Let us not grow weary in well doing."
[GALATIANS 6:9]

Lord, help me to keep going when I would like to stop.

BARBARA PIKULINSKI SURVIVED six years on cancer wards and 20 bouts with reconstructive surgery in order to do something with her life. Her struggle began when she was 14, lasting until she was 20. Now free of cancer, Barbara faces a world with new problems.

Often called "handicapped," she hates the word and doesn't feel it applies to her. She plans to complete college and become a rehabilitation counselor.

"A lot of my friends think I'm dead," the petite 97-pound brunette says. "But you know, I knew I was going to live and do something with my life."

The courage and perseverance of some people put the rest of us to shame. To call them "handicapped" makes the situation doubly ironic.

Barbara Pikulinski thinks of what she can do—and does it. How about you and me?

"What shall a man give in return for his life?"
[MATTHEW 16:26]

❧ Father, may we put our talents to constructive use.

A MUSIC LOVER PAID $14,500 to conduct the Houston, Texas, Symphony Orchestra in one concert.

In a unique fund drive, the Symphony advertised the chance to conduct. Richard Llewellyn Watson, 32-year-old aspiring conductor, came from New York after family and friends chipped in from $2 to $500 each. Mr. Watson, who has a conducting degree from Rome's Conservatory of St. Cecilia, won three standing ovations from the capacity crowd in Houston's Jones Hall.

"Every aspiring conductor wants to have the opportunity to conduct a virtuoso orchestra like this one," he said afterward. Said one orchestra member, "He's better than some of the guest conductors we pay to come here."

Sometimes opportunity knocks. But more often, we have to actively pursue the goals we choose in life.

Being a self-starter doesn't make success inevitable. But it sure makes it more likely.

"Whatever you do, in word or deed, do everything in the name of the Lord."

[COLOSSIANS 3:17]

℮ Lord, motivate us to move ourselves to action.

THE LITTLE VILLAGE of Brimfield, Illinois, population 650, is investing $8,000 so that Jim Ausfahl will become their doctor by 1981.

The Brimfield Area Men's Club has agreed to foot that much of the bill while Jim attends the University of Illinois medical school in Peoria. The 23-year-old student has, in turn, promised to become the community's doctor and to remain for at least five years.

Jim Ausfahl is investing, too—his family's future. "Brimfield was just one of many communities looking for a doctor," he says. "The whole area is doctor poor."

But he believes it will grow enough to support a practice and be the kind of place where he and his wife, Carol, will want to raise their son, Joshua David.

With the severe shortage of medical personnel and the high cost of education, maybe Brimfield's investment is an idea whose time has come.

Does your community need better medical services? What can you—and your neighbors—do about it?

> "The people who know their God shall stand firm and take action." [DANIEL 11:32]

e² Give us, Jesus, a sense of duty towards our family, community and world.

A SECOND CAREER for two New York housewives has meant a second chance for some ex-convicts.

After Dolores Sancetta and Marcia Goldenberg had raised their families, they became theatrical agents. They started an agency, DMI, in Manhattan. They decided to include ex-prisoners among their clients, since acting is a field where talent—not one's past—counts.

Providing ex-cons Chuck Bergansky and Jim White with resumes and introductions to casting directors, DMI helped them break into TV and films. Other clients followed.

"There's a real therapeutic effect in having people see themselves on the screen," says actor and drug rehabilitation counsellor Jim White. "Luckily, my past didn't make any difference."

A second chance is what many people need. A chance to make up for the past, to do better.

God gives us many "second chances." Doesn't that tell us something about how to deal with others?

> "Let us not grow weary in well-doing, for in due season we shall reap, if we do not lose heart." [GALATIANS 6:9]

Widen our vision, Lord, and open our hearts to the feelings and needs of others.

Most intelligent people could be more innovative than they are. *Executives' Digest* lists some characteristics that can stifle creativity:

1. *Excessive need for order*. Inflexible planning can discourage creativity.

2. *A reluctance to play with things, ideas, words, people*. Individuals who are afraid of looking silly rarely innovate.

3. *Resource myopia*. Society values realism—seeing things as they are, whereas innovation requires seeing things as they might be.

4. *Reluctance to risk*. Innovation depends on a willingness to stick one's neck out.

5. *Reluctance to exert influence*. Fear of seeming "pushy" results in acceptance of the established way of doing things, though there might be a better way.

6. *Overcertainty*. The "specialists' disease"—people who really "know" a subject—or think they do—tend to be less open to new approaches.

What's keeping you from being more creative?

> "The purpose in a man's mind is like deep water, but the man of understanding will draw it out." [PROVERBS 20:5]

đ̃ Help me use my ability, Lord, to share in Your work of creation.

At least one 13-year-old boy in New York City is convinced. Jail is not for him.

When the heavy steel door slammed behind him and he looked around the cell and through the bars at dismal corridors, Tony Carson said, "Thank God this ain't real."

Tony was part of a tour sponsored by P.A.L. (Police Athletic League). The program seeks, says one correction official, "to stem the tide of youth who are finding their way into the city prison system."

The boys met Lorence Riley, Jr., 23, once leader of a tough youth gang and now involved in a program designed to keep kids out of gangs and prisons.

"I thought I was superman," he told Tony, who was still in the cell. "Then I ended up in jail."

Help young people to have good experiences: the joy of helping someone; the satisfaction of working with others towards a positive goal. See to it that the youngsters in your life get the right kind of reality.

> "I will do for him whatever seems good."
> [2 SAMUEL 19:38]

ew By my life, Father, may I show others the joy of giving.

SIXTH GRADERS in Cassandra Tyler's class in Atlanta's Garfield school studied "violence on television." They had a lot to report:

"When I see violence on TV I get nightmares," said one boy. Another suggested, "It can be harmful to a lot of people. It can hurt and kill people, but it will also haunt them."

"I wish all the television shows would cut down on violence," wrote one girl. "Some shows have so much it makes me sick." One of her classmates suggested that "people that see these programs are going to view violence as an everyday thing."

Teacher Tyler commented: "Every one of my students watches at least one hour per evening and I feel we have to help them watch critically and evaluate what they see."

Some violence in literature or television is inevitable. It is the context that matters. If you consider a show harmful, turn it off. Let the station manager know your views.

"Judge with right judgment." [JOHN 7:24]

Sharpen our perceptions, Lord, so that we can make better judgments on what we see.

To FAMILY THERAPIST Virginia Satir, every human being is a miracle.

That miracle, says Ms. Satir, an internationally known author and speaker, is always evolving, growing and changing. How the growth and change take place is influenced by how family members see each other.

"Although families can be wonderful things," says the therapist, "they rarely are. Try to know your relatives as people—treat them as real; share love and pain, doubts and criticisms."

She reminds family members that they do not own one another. "The higher the feeling of self-worth," she tells groups, "the less the need for ownership."

Ms. Satir believes that in the 14 countries in which she has conducted workshops, family situations are similar. "Happy families are human, appropriate, flexible."

The family is the foundation of society. What happens between family members doesn't stop there. It is reflected in actions outside the home. It is a matter of loving each member of my family as I love myself.

> "Have we not all one father? Has not one God created us?" [MALACHI 2:10]

ℰℐ Lord, help me to appreciate and contribute to the family you have given me.

To some families, the birth of a mentally retarded "Down's Syndrome" child is a tragedy. But to Duane and Carolyn Mann of Perryville, New York, three adopted Down's babies have brought a houseful of joy.

The Manns had two normal adopted children, Martha, 13, and Daniel, 10, when they decided to add Christina, a 13-month-old Down's baby, to their home. Carolyn had taught retarded children for a time, and had found the youngsters like "a burst of sunshine."

Mark, 2-and-a-half, followed; then Nathaniel, known as Chip, came to the Manns at age 3 months. Both were Down's babies. Like Christina, they are responding well to the warmth and love the Manns give.

"These kids give out a tremendous amount of love," Mr. Mann said. "It's a shame to put them in institutions." He and Carolyn hope to adopt one more child, a little girl, to complete their family.

It may not be possible for you or for me to adopt a child, but each of us can open our hearts—and homes to the unwanted.

"As you did it to one of the least of these My brethren, you did it to Me."

[MATTHEW 25:40]

Help us, Jesus, to give to others the love that You've given to us.

ADULTS IN INCREASING NUMBERS are playing with dollhouses. One expert has called miniature collecting the third biggest hobby in the United States.

A Virginia woman does nothing but make linens for dollhouses. She has so many orders that even with help it will take six months to fill them.

A California man makes models of actual houses. He made 15 models of a Victorian house in Alameda, sold all 15 and has orders for other models that will keep him busy for the next two years.

A St. Louis author and journalist made a dollhouse for her daughters. Now she publishes a newsletter for miniature collectors with a subscription list of people all over the world, and has written three books on dollhouses and furnishings.

Why do tiny things have such fascination for so many people? Perhaps things in small scale seem more manageable—we can control them better than the elements of ordinary life.

In any case, play is important in life. Encourage it.

"God richly furnishes us with everything to enjoy."   [1 TIMOTHY 6:17]

ếć   May we lighten our lives and that of others, Lord, with simple fun.

WHY ARE BARBERS, BARTENDERS and beauticians successful "poor men's psychiatrists"? A study by Dr. Eugene Gauron of the University of Iowa cites these abilities:

- He or she helps the other person focus on the important aspect of whatever is bothering him.
- The helping person becomes a kind of middleman, getting the problem in perspective and suggesting another way of looking at it.
- The good paraprofessional can listen with sympathetic gestures and mannerisms. People are still reluctant to get help for mental illness. The helping person goes a long way toward overcoming such fears.

If we care about people and develop skills such as listening and being objective, any of us can be a real help.

How much do any of us want to enter into the problems of another? God stands ready to help us go as far as we are able.

"Be ready to listen."   [SIRACH 6:35]

&ε&   Make us quick to listen, Lord, slow to judge
       and even slower to condemn.

IF YOUR DAY SEEMS to keep getting shorter, you may have fallen into a "time trap" says Dr. Alec MacKenzie in his seminar for women in management.

Dr. MacKenzie lists 150 time wasters, from over-long telephone calls to poor organization. They are particularly important to women, he claims, because "when a woman goes to work there is often the tacit assumption that she will also still manage the home."

Dr. MacKenzie suggests that women holding the two jobs cut back on housekeeping and give family members more systematic household tasks. He says, "A woman must do as well in the office as her competition, often a man who is holding only one job."

If we're not getting done all we set out to do, we can either lower our expectations or increase our efficiency. Either way, we first have to slow down and think. A little thought may help free you from the "time trap."

"He has appointed a time for every matter and for every work." [ECCLESIASTES 3:17]

Don't let us forget, Lord, that just because we're on the go, it doesn't mean we're going the right way.

Toys ARE NOT just "kid stuff," according to Dr. Henry Levinstein, a physics professor who teaches "The Physical Basis of Toys" at New York's Syracuse University.

In a "toy lab" with over 500 dolls, trains, music boxes, planes and puzzles, Dr. Levinstein's students learn the scientific principles used in mechanical toys and study what makes a toy fun for kids.

Dr. Levinstein feels that "anything that amuses" a child is a good toy. He believes that many toys are poorly made and don't do anything. He believes that a toy's role "shouldn't be so much teaching as helping develop skill and coordination."

Skill and coordination are good qualities to achieve. So are wisdom, compassion and sensitivity. Like all skills, they require long practice.

The extent to which any of us is a child of God may be measured by the degree of love we show other people. Work at it.

> "Even as I have loved you ... love one another." [JOHN 13:34]

ﷺ Put us in touch with our inner selves, Holy Spirit, and lead us to act under Your guidance.

A WOMAN WITH A UNIQUE decorating flair discovered a business opportunity—and is bringing financial bonanzas to others, as well.

Micheline Masse founded Stock Market Information Service, Inc. of Montreal, in 1969 when she learned that old stock she planned to use to wallpaper a room was worth several thousand dollars. She quickly changed her mind and became a stock tracer—at $20.00 a search.

Her most successful client is a retired U.S. naval officer. In the 1930's, he bought 1,000 shares of oil stock for 25¢ a share. He had been holding it "as a souvenir." "It's a fairy tale," he says. "Today it's worth $42,000!"

"I was so lucky myself," says Miss Masse. "I wanted to help others!"

If we hug our benefits to ourselves, we stand to lose what we thought we gained. But if we are open-handed, we can be a source of material and even spiritual gain to others—and ourselves. Happiness grows by giving it away.

"Rejoice with me."   [LUKE 15:6]

ℰ   Direct our thoughts and actions in an outgoing way, Holy Spirit, and not merely toward ourselves.

READERS OF THE NATION'S largest weekly news and sports magazines recently saw a large ad with the message, "God cares about you, wants to be your friend."

The ad was part of a campaign by 15 Protestant churches "to reach the average, middle-class guy who, by decision or default, is turned off." Says the Rev. Robert Barr of Rochester, New York, one of the participating ministers, "We want to turn him on; tell him he's missing something."

Time, Newsweek, Sports Illustrated and *U.S. News and World Report* were chosen for the regional ads because of their wide coverage and the respect they enjoy. The messages were directed to the lonely, the confused and those who feel a lack in their lives.

Many people feel they are "missing something" in their lives. And a proper understanding of the role of Jesus Christ in our lives may be just what they're looking for. He can be found by those who seek Him, in prayer, in silence and in acting as He did.

"When you seek Me with all your heart, I will be found by you." [JEREMIAH 29:13,14]

Help us to look for You, Jesus, in the events of our daily lives.

BUNNELL, FLORIDA (Pop. 1,500), may have the youngest police chief in the United States. He's Donald Brock. And he's 19 years old.

"The biggest problem we're facing is keeping the juvenile crime rate down," says the chief of Bunnell's six-member police force. "There is no organized recreation for teenagers in this city or county, and with nothing to do, the kids turn to crime."

Chief Brock is a graduate of Bunnell High. He has taken 400 hours of police training at Daytona Beach Community College.

"The only thing we can do," he told the community, "is start working with the kids, but the law can't do it alone. As long as we work together, we won't have any problems."

Working together can solve many problems. It can often make big ones smaller. It can help make just about any problem more manageable.

Who could use your cooperation—today?

> "I would have you wise as to what is good and guileless as to what is evil." [ROMANS 16:19]

ҿ⃗ Spirit of love, show us ways in which we may work together for the good of all.

An Alpine winter sports holiday is the dream of many skiers, but the dream is becoming a nightmare.

A new ecology group in Innsbruck, Austria, warns that the spread of hotels, condominiums, ski slopes and lifts is causing grave damage to vegetation, wildlife, water supplies and the landscape.

"The time has come to limit further growth of winter sports and tourism in the Alps," said Government professor Siegbert Morscher, a spokesman for ecologists in the Tyrol. They point out that Austria, two-thirds the size of New York State, has 5,000 ski lifts and 15,000 man-made ski trails. In some runs the soil's capacity to store water has decreased by 90 percent. Erosion follows with serious harm to plant life.

There is a balance in creation that requires our respect. Natural resources are not limitless, but they can last if used wisely. Often alternatives can be found. Be a steward, not a squanderer.

> "Turn in the account of your stewardship, for you can no longer be steward." [LUKE 16:2]

Holy Spirit, help me to think straight.

A COLLEGE STUDENT who cycled for three months across the country is writing thank-you letters to 60 families who befriended him.

David Schwartz, 21, had taken off from his home in Brooklyn and headed for California. He would pedal all day and in the evening knock at the door of a house, asking if he could pitch his tent in the owner's yard or field.

Usually they offered him a room, accepted his help with chores and often offered extra food or money as he left. Delighted, he said, "Strangers accepted me as I am."

We tend to be suspicious of strangers but, in David Schwartz's experience, Americans still live up to their reputation of being open and generous.

Let us hope the high incidence of crime and the fear it generates are not making us a people withdrawn, grim, scared of our own shadows.

While we should not take foolish risks, if we reach out in trust, we may find for ourselves the goodness in people.

> "Let brotherly love continue. Do not neglect to show hospitality to strangers."
> [HEBREWS 13:1,2]

ट Lord, help me trust in people's goodness instead of suspecting them.

A SUBORDINATE HAS FLOWN into a rage because he feels he was not consulted on a major policy change.

Your secretary is quitting because you criticized her too harshly.

International Management points out a common denominator in these situations: the people involved are tense—thus over-sensitive and low in objectivity and perspective. To defuse the tension, try this:

- Concede any points you can. Concede that there is a problem.
- Apologize if it is at all appropriate.
- Listen. Your self-control may be contagious.
- Set a future date to discuss the issue.
- Leave, if you must. If your own emotions are out of hand, this may be the wiser course.

The above situations translate into life at home, at school, wherever human beings are together. If you try to defuse the tension, you will be sure of at least your own control. And that's a start.

> "Anxiety in a man's heart weighs him down,
> but a good word makes him glad."
>
> [PROVERBS 12:25]

Holy Spirit, may I open myself to Your Love so that it may fill my being.

ALTHOUGH ALMOST 50,000 blind people in the United States would have a chance of regaining their sight through corneal transplants, eye banks can help only a tenth of that number.

"We're only getting about 3,000 corneas a year," says Frederick Griffith, director of the Medical Eye Bank of Maryland, the world's largest. "If only people would bequeath their corneas—not even the whole eye—to any of the 69 eye banks we have in the United States, we could prevent a great deal of blindness."

The gift of sight, says Mr. Griffiths, is the least a person can leave, and something that can bring new light to another person's life.

Each of us can give this gift of sight.

If you decide that you want to do this, contact your local Eye Bank. They will send you a small identification card to carry in your wallet. It's as simple as that.

> "And the blind man said to Him...'Let me receive my sight.'" [MARK 10:51]

ᏋᏝ Inspire us, Holy Spirit, to be generous with ourselves in death as in life.

IF YOU NEED A VACATION, how about going to a sane asylum?

Dr. Darold A. Treffert, director of the Winnebago Mental Health Institute in Wisconsin thinks the "worried well" should have a place to take it easy so they don't become the "worried sick."

"We subsidize a huge amount of resources," he says, such as crisis centers, emergency rooms and halfway houses, "which are really alternatives to asylums."

Why not, says Dr. Treffert, have an "asylum" for people who are approaching their private breaking points? He envisions a place where one could take part in crafts, lectures, therapy or do nothing at all.

Why wait until we reach our own breaking points before taking a break?

We rest our eyes by looking into the distance. Mind, body and spirit relax when we take time out to look beyond the immediate to a larger vision: a prayer, poetry, the Scriptures, a personal goal. Try it frequently.

> "Go in peace. The journey on which you go is
> under the eye of the Lord." [JUDGES 18:6]

     May I lift my eyes to You, Lord, and find the peace You have promised.

DOES THE BILL OF RIGHTS provide sufficient protection for all Americans? Eunice Kennedy Shriver thinks not. She feels that retarded persons—between two and six million people—need something more.

Mrs. Shriver, long an advocate for the retarded, pointed out that bills have been introduced in several state legislatures that would permit euthanasia and sterilization of the retarded.

Only some explicit recognition of the rights of these citizens, she feels, can guarantee retardees some security regarding the "life, liberty and pursuit of happiness" the rest of us tend to take for granted.

If anyone's rights are endangered—whether by government decree or by an individual—how safe can any of us be?

Like everybody else, retarded persons can do certain things and cannot do others. Like everyone else, they are human beings entitled to respect and the protection of the law. Do what you can to see that they get it.

> "As you did it to one of the least of these, My brethren, you did it to Me."
>
> [MATTHEW 25:40]

  Father, may I respect the worth of each of my brothers and sisters.

A CALIFORNIA BUSINESSMAN was on the receiving end of honesty.

On one of his visits to New York City, he lost his wallet. Much to his surprise, the desk clerk handed it to him when he returned to his hotel.

A man—who didn't even leave his name—had found the wallet in the neighborhood. He had then canvassed several hotels until he located the one in which the businessman was registered. Everything in the wallet was intact.

It should be usual to find honesty. But is it? Wouldn't it be wonderful if everyone cared about his neighbor?

In our dealings with others, are we always respectful of their property, their rights, their needs? Are we worthy of their trust? Our caring should go beyond material objects, and our honesty beyond money. Honesty should be present in all our relationships. We are all brothers.

"Then the righteous will shine like the sun in the kingdom of their Father."

[MATTHEW 13:43]

Lord, help us to appreciate our brothers' virtues and to forget their imperfections.

THE STRANGEST MEDICAL prescription ever written may be a tiny space suit to keep David, a 6-year-old Houston, Texas, youngster in germ-free isolation.

David, whose family name is kept secret by Texas Children's Hospital and Baylor College of Medicine, is part of the most dramatic human experiment ever performed. Born with a rare genetic immune deficiency, he was isolated in a sterile chamber until the suit was devised. Now after six years, he is free to run and play, cling to and hug others, and explore beyond his plastic chamber.

Said Dr. John Montgomery, "We never thought we'd see him reach age six in isolation. There has been enough spin-off from David scientifically to justify all the efforts and effects, not to mention the fact that he is alive, he is well and has never been sick, he is happy, and living a reasonably normal life. Would I do it again? Absolutely."

One idea gives birth to another. Don't overlook any chance to communicate good ideas. The results may surprise you.

> "He gave skill to men ... by them He heals and takes away pain."   [SIRACH 38:6,7]

🙏 Lord, help me to realize that I can make a difference—make things better.

Thirty mentally retarded women received a very special Christmas gift—the feeling of looking pretty.

The 20 staff members of a local beauty salon gave their talents, their day off and the full beauty treatment to women of the Baltimore Association for Retarded Citizens.

Julie, 27, couldn't wait to show her freshly styled hair, painted nails and new face to her best friend. Asked what she enjoyed most, she replied shyly, "All you beautiful people."

"They just want to be cared for and loved," said shop-owner Gloria Brennan. She added, "Looking good is such an important part of feeling good."

It was a long day. But, said Miss Brennan, "Twelve months will go by, and we'll do it again."

Giving others a feeling that you care isn't hard to do. Caring shows itself in very small, everyday gestures. Just notice what your spouse, a child, a friend, a neighbor likes or needs. Form a caring habit.

"Have the same care for one another."
[1 CORINTHIANS 12:25]

Help me, Lord, to be sensitive to the unspoken needs of others.

Ⓝewborn babies are sensitive, feeling people, says Scottish psychoanalyst Dr. R.D. Laing in his film "Birth, with R.D. Laing."

In the film, Dr. Laing pleads for more humane, "less surgical" delivery procedures, both for mother and baby. Says Dr. Laing, "We should welcome babies with kindness and respect. An infant has all its sense channels open and is not a lump of stuff to be turned upside down and slapped."

Dr. Laing feels that preserving the mother-baby relationship is critical in the first 72 hours of life, the time they most need each other. "It's the shattering of these bonds that's a precondition of insanity," he feels. He is certain that humane treatment of infants can have a positive effect on their mental health as adults.

The mental health of a person is supported when he or she is "welcomed with kindness and respect." It is what we want for ourselves; do we extend the same treatment to others?

"Show kindness." [ZECHARIAH 7:9]

ⅇℯ Inspire in us, Jesus, a deep respect for each other.

WHEN PERSONALITIES CLASH, are you a mediator or an arbitrator? There's a big difference, says the Organizational Behavior Institute.

● Arbitration lays down the law. Mediation changes the situation.

● The mediator stays neutral. The arbitrator resolves the problem by fiat, leaving scars.

● The arbitrator takes one side, and puts down the other. The mediator sets ground rules demanding mutual respect and open listening.

Mediation stresses data, sees that the opponents have access to one another's facts. The mediator recognizes that they are haggling from separate isolations and tries to open them to the big picture.

The mediator, says the Institute, is "the hearing aid for people who are deaf with rage."

Every organization needs mediators. And that includes the family, as any parent knows.

But often just two people are alone in their "deafness." At least one has to listen. Can you?

"An attentive ear is the wise man's desire."
[SIRACH 3:29]

● Help us, Lord, to remove the barriers of self-ishness that keeps us from really listening to others.

THE INVENTOR of earmuffs might have gone unremembered without a boost from the State of Maine.

The legislature, deciding the move would "bolster the tradition of warmth from Franklin County," voted to rescue the local inventor from obscurity by designating the first day of winter each year as Chester Greenwood Day.

Mr. Greenwood, born in Franklin County, Maine, in 1858, designed "Champion Ear Protectors," better known as earmuffs.

Did Chester Greenwood know that his "ear protectors" would be such a boon to human kind? Probably not. But they were a good idea, and he carried that idea to a successful conclusion.

You and I can't know what long-range effect our good ideas will have—not usually. But that's hardly an excuse for refusing to light a candle rather than curse the darkness. In fact, it's a good reason to try.

"Cast off the works of darkness and put on the armour of light."   [ROMANS 13:12]

Holy Spirit, make us creative in meeting each day's challenges.

"**C**ONSPICUOUS CONSUMPTION" MAY be on the way out. In some restaurants, portions are being whittled down for those who choose to eat less.

Camelback Inn in Scottsdale, Arizona, cooperated with the Department of Agriculture in a recent study. They offered three sirloin steak sizes and both six-and four-piece portions of baked shrimp. Seventy percent chose the smaller and less expensive steak portions. Sixty-five percent ordered fewer shrimp.

Other restaurants are beginning to follow suit. This may be a small revolution in our eating-out habits. The deciding factor, of course, will be the consumer.

Heavy consumption, says James W. McLamore, president of the National Restaurant Association, "may be giving way to a current ethic of 'conspicuous conservation.'"

Stewardship—thoughtful use and conservation of God's creation—is an old idea. Maybe, it is once again an idea whose time has come. If you want, you can help speed the process.

> "Who then is the faithful and wise steward whom the master will set over his household?"
> [LUKE 12:42]

Father, may we be good and faithful stewards of Your gifts.

DRUNK DRIVERS ARE never a laughing matter, says recovered alcoholic Betty Kiddle, an Alcoholics Anonymous staffer. She urges party hosts to take these steps to help the life of the party stay alive:

- Serve foods that slow the rate of alcohol absorption—cheese and crackers, dips, fondues, eggs.
- Have jiggers so guests can measure their drinks.
- Use a tea or fruit juice base for punch. Carbonated mixers cause fast absorption of alcohol.
- Don't rush to refill guests' glasses. People often accept drinks only to avoid seeming rude.
- Stop serving alcohol an hour before the party ends. Switch to coffee or non-alcoholic drinks.
- If a guest is obviously drunk, arrange a ride or call a cab. Risk losing a friend and take the car keys if you have to. It may prevent tragedy.

We wouldn't be likely to invite people to a party without making plans for their enjoyment and comfort. A little extra effort can provide for something far more important—their safety.

> "Act accordingly, that you may be kept in safety." [SIRACH 3:1]

Jesus, encourage us to take that extra step to care for others.

AFTER A BURGLARY of his wife's jewelry, Peter James Lee, a North Carolina minister, put this letter, addressed to the thief, in the Chapel Hill newspaper:

"...You now have the old ring Kristy's grandfather gave her grandmother in Norway before they came to America...But you can never have the love, the memories that ring has symbolized for decades...

"You have the tiny cross our daughter's godmother gave to her at her baptism. But you can never have the cherishing that went with it.

"You have just about every trinket, ring, little stone that I have given to Kristy on birthdays, anniversaries, and Christmases past. But you have never seen her eyes when she opened the gifts for the first time...

"You have our finest things. But you can never have our treasures. They remain in our hearts, not locked, not protected, but there to share in love."

It hurts to lose a cherished object. But there is joy in the sharpened awareness that your real treasure can't be taken away. A reminder to love more.

> "For where your treasure is, there will your heart be also."   [MATTHEW 6:21]

℘ Holy Spirit, may we have the discernment each day to recognize what is really to be cherished.

Ⅰт was probably Jimmy Mahoney's most important Christmas.

A Marine, he had been married shortly before going overseas in World War II. He and his wife had never had a chance to celebrate Christmas together.

On Christmas Eve, 1945, he was on his way home, planning to stop to buy a special present for his wife. Grounded planes and cancelled flights caused him to arrive long after stores had closed.

Mournfully, he took a cab from the airport. Then he saw a drugstore open, stopped and made a purchase. When he finally rang the doorbell of his apartment, his wife opened the door and saw her gift.

There he stood with a large red ribbon and bow across his chest, and a card which read, "To Mary from Jimmy, with all my love."

We do a lot of fussing about Christmas preparation. We become immersed in selecting and wrapping Christmas packages. How many of us give those we love what they really want—ourselves?

> "Owe no one anything, except to love one another." [ROMANS 13:8]

ċ²   Holy Spirit, teach us to give the gift of ourselves.

A Jew who was under torture in a Nazi concentration camp wrote a prayer which included these words:

"Peace be to men of bad will, and an end to all
revenge and to all words of pain and punishment...
So many have borne witness with their blood!
O God, do not put their suffering upon the scales
of Thy justice,
Lest it be counted to the hangman...
But to all hangmen and informers, to all traitors
and evil ones, do grant the benefit of the
courage and fortitude shown by those others,
who were their victims...
May this be the ransom that restores justice.
And all that is good, let it be counted
and all that is evil, let it be wiped out...
May peace come once more upon this earth,
peace to men of good will; and may it descend
upon the others also. Amen."

A man named Stephen, a disciple of the crucified Jesus of Nazareth, was condemned to death by stoning. As he died, he too said, "Lord, do not hold this sin against them." One of his persecutors who was standing by was Saul of Tarsus. We know him as St. Paul.

AROUND CHRISTMAS time, *The New York Times* printed this letter from a reader:

"One day recently, I entered the chapel of the Presbyterian Church at 55th Street and Fifth Avenue...I saw the bent figures of two 'bag women,' who are familiar sights in the neighborhood, sleeping quietly out of the cold. Their possessions, in worn shopping bags, were at their feet.

"Another woman entered the dim chapel, dignified, well-dressed. After finishing her prayers, I saw her catch sight of the two poorly dressed women. Then she opened her pocketbook and took out a couple of bills.

"She walked to the pew in which the bag women were dozing and placed the money on the cushions almost under their hands, and walked out, smiling."

"What you do to one of My least brethren, you do to Me," Jesus said 2,000 years ago. But the lesson has lost none of its urgency. What have you done for your brother and sister in need recently?

"Stretch forth your hand to the poor, so that your blessing may be complete."

[SIRACH 7:32]

Lord, may our love show itself in action.

THERE'S MORE THAN ONE way to a college degree. Donald Mandery goes to class on the Long Island Railroad while he commutes to work in New York City.

Mr. Mandery has gotten his bachelor of arts degree via the Edu-Tran/Adelphi-on-Wheels program and is en route to a master's in business administration.

With a four-semester plan, a student can take two courses a term (six credits) and have 24 credits at the end of the year. And he can hold a full-time job.

This way, says Mr. Mandery, "I'm home for dinner every night... I arrive home at my normal time and can still prepare my assignments due for the next day... This program also allows me to see my family."

If the student can't go to the classroom, there's a lot to be said for bringing the classroom to the student—even on tracks.

Your community has many educational resources. Are they really serving the community? Can you help them do it better?

"An intelligent mind acquires knowledge, and the ear of the wise seeks knowledge."
[PROVERBS 18:15]

Holy Spirit, guide those seeking to make our schools more effective.

ANDREW DAVIS HAS BECOME a cave man to fight the high cost of living.

When Mr. Davis got a $167 bill for one month's heat in his Armington, Illinois, home, he told his family, "We're going to move into a cave."

Mr. Davis bought two lots against a hillside and dug his cave home. The home has two baths, three large bedrooms, a 32-foot-long living room, kitchen and sauna room, with indirect lighting from a wind-powered electrical generator. The temperature is a steady 58 degrees, with additional heat in winter from a fireplace with circulating fan.

"I won't need insurance, it can't burn down," says Mr. Davis. "There's no roof to paint, no gutters to clean, no windows to replace, no painting to do and no worry about tornadoes."

One cave man can hardly be called a trend. But there's need for all of us to reduce energy consumption. We don't have to imitate what someone does. But we can learn from it.

> "If there is any excellence, if there is anything worthy of praise, think about these things."
> [PHILIPPIANS 4:8]

ଏଏ Father, help us to learn from the experience of others.

ONE CHRISTMAS, Phyllis Brienza, a waitress at the Bun & Burger in New York, received a card signed, "Medium rare, pressed." She knew exactly who it was from.

It's this instant recognition that makes Mrs. Brienza so special to her "regulars." One man walks in and she calls, without hesitation, "medium with half a bun and French."

"With a memory like yours," said the customer to Mrs. Brienza, "you can have a job in my office any time."

The woman next to him added, "It's flattering to have one's little eccentricities remembered. I like the fact that she knows me, even if it's only as a 'medium rare, no bun, side of French, slice of lemon.'"

Chances are, it's not just a matter of good memory, but of caring enough to make the effort.

Caring makes the difference between "getting the job done" and giving quality to your work. It's an ingredient that can change lives, yours, and others'.

> "Love one another with brotherly affection;
> outdo one another in showing honor."
> [ROMANS 12:10]

ಆ Help me, Lord, to remember that creation is still going on—that I can help to make it a better world.

Do SOMETHING SPECIAL today. And again tomorrow:
Mend a quarrel.
Seek out a forgotten friend.
Write a love letter.
Share a treasure.
Encourage a young person.
Keep a promise.
Find the time.
Forego a grudge. Forgive someone.
Listen.
Apologize if you were wrong.
Try to understand that certain person.
Examine your demands on someone.
Appreciate.
Be kind. Be gentle.
Laugh a little. Laugh a little more.
Welcome a stranger.
Gladden the heart of a child.
Take pleasure in the beauty and wonder of the earth.
Speak your love. Speak it again. Speak it still again.

"Let all that you do be done in love."
[1 CORINTHIANS 16:14]

Lord, may we keep our lives vital by breaking out of the pattern each day.